Straw Dogs

D0715749

✖ Controversies

Series editors: Stevie Simkin and Julian Petley

Controversies is a series comprising individual studies of controversial films from the late 1960s to the present day, encompassing classic, contemporary Hollywood, cult and world cinema. Each volume provides an in-depth study analysing the various stages of each film's production, distribution, classification and reception, assessing both its impact at the time of its release and its subsequent legacy.

Also published

Neal King, *The Passion of the Christ*

Shaun Kimber, *Henry: Portrait of a Serial Killer*

Peter Krämer, *A Clockwork Orange*

Forthcoming

Lucy Burke, *The Idiots*

Gabrielle Murray, *Bad Boy Bubby*

Jude Davies, *Falling Down*

Julian Petley, *Crash*

Stevie Simkin, *Basic Instinct*

'The *Controversies* series is a valuable contribution to the ongoing debate about what limits – if any – should be placed on cinema when it comes to the depiction and discussion of extreme subject matter. Sober, balanced and insightful where much debate on these matters has been hysterical, one-sided and unhelpful, these books should help us get a perspective on some of the thorniest films in the history of cinema.'
Kim Newman, novelist, critic and broadcaster

Straw Dogs

Stevie Simkin

palgrave
macmillan

© Stevie Simkin 2011

First published 2011 by
PALGRAVE MACMILLAN

PALGRAVE MACMILLAN in the UK is an imprint of Macmillan Publishers Limited, registered in England, company number 785998, of Houndmills, Basingstoke, Hampshire RG21 6XS.

Palgrave Macmillan in the US is a division of St Martin's Press LLC, 175 Fifth Avenue, New York, NY 10010.

Palgrave Macmillan is the global academic imprint of the above companies and has companies and representatives throughout the world.

Palgrave® and Macmillan® are registered trademarks in the United States, the United Kingdom, Europe and other countries

ISBN: 978–0–230–29670–1

This book is printed on paper suitable for recycling and made from fully managed and sustained forest sources. Logging, pulping and manufacturing processes are expected to conform to the environmental regulations of the country of origin.

A catalogue record for this book is available from the British Library.

A catalog record for this book is available from the Library of Congress.

10   9   8   7   6   5   4   3   2   1
20   19   18   17   16   15   14   13   12   11

Printed in China

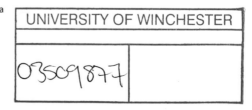

For Sophie

Contents

Part 3: Key Themes and Ideas

Part 4: Key Scene Analysis

Part 5: The Legacy of *Straw Dogs*

Appendices

Acknowledgements

I am grateful to Jenny Romero and the staff at the Margaret Herrick Library, Los Angeles for their assistance during an intensive four-day immersion in the Sam Peckinpah Collection. Thanks are also due to the staff at the offices of the BBFC, in particular Edward Lamberti, for his help in accessing the relevant files there and dealing with permissions, and Craig Lapper for his detailed responses to my questions. Thank you to Nathalie Morris and the staff at the British Film Institute Library for help with archive materials, including the James Ferman Collection.

At the University of Winchester, I am grateful to the Research and Knowledge Exchange Committee in the Faculty of Arts for granting a short period of research leave to complete the first draft of the book, and for funding the trip to Los Angeles for essential archive research.

Friends and colleagues who were particularly helpful in exchanges of ideas include Helen Grime, Marianne Sharp, Nick Joseph, Tom Andrew-Power and, as always, Rob Conkie. A special thank you to Brian Woolland who read and annotated the whole manuscript, raising all the most difficult, most important questions along the way.

Invaluable insights were provided by Peter Woods, who was most generous with his time and his own research archive. I am grateful in particular for his input on the details of the film's tortuous final journey to home-video certification in the UK. I would also like to extend my thanks to Katy Haber, Garner Simmons, David Weddle and Stephen Farber for informative email exchanges.

Amongst my *Controversies* colleagues, Peter Kramer gave extensive feedback on an early complete draft. My thanks to him are also due for his crucial input on the series itself. Julian Petley has been a strong driving force behind the series and I have benefited greatly from his wisdom, experience and invaluable work as co-editor.

Thanks to our editor at Palgrave Macmillan, Rebecca Barden, for her faith in the series and her advice throughout. Thanks also to Paul Sng, and to Chantal Latchford for her careful attention to detail in editing the manuscript.

I would also like to thank the students who have taken the undergraduate module 'Body Parts: Early Modern Tragedy and the Cinema of Violence' at the University of Winchester. Over the twelve years or so I have taught it, there have been at least 400 of them. *Straw Dogs* has been a part of the syllabus throughout, and the discussions have never been less than fascinating. These pages bear their heavy imprint.

Finally, thanks and love to my family, as ever, for their forbearance, and for the joy they bring: Aileen, Jamie, Matthew and Sophie.

A Note on References

In the interests of clarity and simplicity, the References Appendix is split into three sections: Section 1 consists of books, essays, articles and reviews, including internet sources. Section 2 consists of archive sources drawn from the Sam Peckinpah Collection held at the Margaret Herrick Library, Los Angeles. References in the text to the archive are preceded by the abbreviation 'SPC' (Sam Peckinpah Collection); some names are then abbreviated to initials for the sake of fluency, so that 'Goodman & Peckinpah' is abbreviated to 'G&P', etc. Numbers and letters in square brackets in the list of references in Section 2 refer to the Peckinpah archive folders. Section 3 lists sources from the archive of the British Board of Film Classification (BBFC). In the text, these references are preceded with the lower-case initials 'bbfc'. Upper-case 'BBFC' references are linked to items listed in Section 1 (online documents from the Board's website). Section 4 provides information about the DVDs referred to in the course of the discussion.

✕ Introduction

When Peckinpah asked his biographer Garner Simmons why he had chosen to write a book about him, Simmons replied that he believed that few films can stand the test of time, but that he thought several of Peckinpah's 'would still be shown as long as there was a way to project images on a screen'. Peckinpah, shaking his head, replied: '"Bullshit. I'm just a good whore. I go where I'm kicked"' (Simmons, 1998, p. xxiv). In itself, it's an exchange of little consequence, perhaps: a biographer and fan expressing sincere admiration, and the director responding with typical acerbic self-deprecation. However, as I prepare to offer analysis of a film now celebrating its fortieth anniversary, it raises useful questions about the canon of classic film. Times change, and with them, horizons of expectation, reception, and notions of what is 'acceptable' and 'unacceptable'. In other respects, however, it is possible to see our culture moving not on linear tracks but rather through cycles, and all of this is directly relevant to an understanding of how *Straw Dogs* still retains its power to shock and disturb four decades after it was first screened.

My contention is that many of the most fascinating aspects of *Straw Dogs* come to life when we assess its significance in its original context, *in parallel with* a consideration of its impact on audiences today. Our current understanding of the film is conditioned by the impact of massive social and political revolutions, particularly in terms of the perceived, represented and actual positions of women in Western society. In some senses, the changes represent a literal, complete revolution: at a time when what Ariel Levy terms 'raunch culture' is more prevalent than ever (2005), when popular culture is once again routinely commodifying female sexuality for heterosexual male consumption, it may be that Western sexual politics is currently closer to the

1970s norm than it was, say, fifteen years ago, and this puts us in a complex position when considering the film's representation of sexuality.

Straw Dogs tells the story of an American academic, David Sumner, and his young British wife Amy returning to her hometown in Cornwall. Their arrival ignites suspicion and hostility in this closeknit community, as well as jealousies and tensions that finally erupt in a sexual assault on Amy by two of the villagers, including her former lover Charlie Venner. The film builds to a violent climax when an armed posse of five villagers besieges the Sumners' farmhouse, forcing the pacifist David to abandon his principles and engage in a brutal struggle for survival.

Inevitably, the discussion in this book will centre on the rape scene which is at the heart of the controversy that has raged and stormed around the film over the past forty years. The scene, the circumstances surrounding it, and the ways in which it has been interpreted and debated over the decades, are complex, and it is important to negotiate the territory with care, and with a full awareness of its contexts, particularly in terms of history and gender politics. In line with the structure of the book and the *Controversies* series more generally, the scene will be considered in terms of the production of the film itself first; it will then be explored in a wider-ranging discussion of the film's impact on contemporaneous audiences and critics, with particular attention paid to the significance of feminist responses. Debate about the scene and its potentially harmful effects on male viewers in particular has informed deliberations over censorship of the film in the UK, and this is covered in the next section, which traces the strange passage of *Straw Dogs* in its transfer to videotape in the 1980s and then to optical media such as DVD in the 90s and into the new millennium. Finally, there is a close discussion of the scene, with particular attention paid to technical aspects and their implications, in the Key Scene Analysis section.

However, a preoccupation with the sexual violence for which *Straw Dogs* is most often remembered can obscure the fact that it is a movie that was conceived, written and made in the shadow of the Vietnam War, as well as in the wider context of the sexual revolution, the rise of the counterculture, and the massive social upheavals of the period: the Civil Rights movement, the activities of the Black Panthers and other groups, the emergence of the women's liberation movement, and, in the following year (1968), the assassinations of Robert Kennedy and Martin Luther King. These significant elements inform the discussion in Parts 1 and 3.

In my own experience discussing *Straw Dogs* with students, most of whom were born twenty years after the film was made, there have always been a number of issues to be negotiated. First – if mundanely – I find myself having to deal with the expectations they bring to a notoriously violent film, banned on home video in the UK for eighteen years. Raised on a film grammar that favours frenetic editing, narrative elision and bold character strokes, the subtlety of characterisation, steady pace, careful narrative plotting and slow-rising tension of Peckinpah's movie can make it difficult for them to engage with it as readily as one might expect.[1] Often it requires a conscious effort on their part to tune into its cinematic language. Once past the first hurdle, I need to find ways to facilitate discussion of the film's representations of violence and sexuality. For some, the overriding response is bewilderment; how could such a tame film, they wonder, have caused so much controversy? Closer discussion of the rape scene invites comparison with subsequent attempts to represent sexual assault on film, notably *The Accused* (1988) and *Irreversible* (2002). Some students are also familiar with more obscure rape-revenge movies such as *I Spit on Your Grave* (1978) and *The Last House on the Left* (1972).[2] The rape scenes in these films are unquestionably more violent and graphic, sometimes even more protracted. However, it rarely takes long for the particularly troubling aspects of the *Straw Dogs* scene to make themselves apparent in discussion. The scene's gender politics often give rise to frank and strongly worded exchanges of views.

All this constitutes a useful reminder that controversies of film censorship and certification are rarely straightforward. Crucial decisions that affect a population's ability to access a particular film are made by small groups of people put in positions of great responsibility. Those decisions are influenced by a wide array of factors – press campaigns, news reports, discussions between censors and film-makers. Of course, the passing of time is another significant element. Today, films routinely certified '15' in the UK, particularly in the horror genre, would, without a doubt, have been awarded '18' certificates ten years ago: thirty years before that, the graphic violence that is a particular feature of these films would have been unacceptable, and quite possibly unimaginable, to those working at the offices of the BBFC and the Motion Picture Association of America (MPAA). Furthermore, it is not only the bodies handed the onerous task of certification and censorship that are important: usually the film-makers are themselves aware of the controversies they are stepping into as they write, prepare, shoot and edit their movies. Controversy inheres in the production process itself, and a full understanding of the film in question remains beyond us if we choose to ignore the circumstances, conditions, choices and decisions that made the film what it is.

Straw Dogs is a clear case in point. The folders of the Sam Peckinpah Collection, held at the Margaret Herrick Library in Los Angeles, contain a staggering array of documents, including multiple draft screenplays, sheaves of pages with corrections and additions, memos, letters and cables, script, production and meeting notes, contracts, bills and call sheets, and copies of contemporaneous interviews, articles and reviews. They give startling insights into the film-making process, and illuminate and sometimes challenge the stories that have gathered around this particular stage of Peckinpah's career – a director whose whole life was prone to snowballing myths and legends. The current study, capitalising on these resources, favours a two-pronged approach to the film. The initial focus is on the making of the film, and, equally important, the context in which it was produced, marketed and then consumed by its first audiences. No amount of research can ever open a direct route into the mind of the director as his vision took shape, and came to life on set; in the final analysis, the finished film exists as a work of art in its own right, sufficient in itself. Nevertheless, a closer look at the history of the making of the movie, including its early drafts, records of meetings and rehearsals, and the interaction of director, cast and crew during shooting, can be revealing. Furthermore, the attempt to parse the truth from the fiction might tell us more about the interaction between the film itself and its accrued mythology.

The second aim is to understand how the film's meanings evolved in the years that followed. The general pattern for the reception of films that challenge or transgress social taboos is a flurry of controversy, and a gradual tailing off as attitudes shift, and, frequently, as other films emerge to push even harder against boundaries of taste and notions of what is and is not acceptable. This has not been the case for *Straw Dogs*. The film's long, strange trip – from its inception, through script development, pre-production, shooting, post-production and release, and on to its even more unusual journey to home-video release – is a revealing one. Challenged by one offended viewer, Peckinpah thanked her for her comments, and responded: 'I didn't want you to enjoy the film. I wanted you to look very close at your own soul' (SPC Peckinpah, 1972a). A close study of the film, through the deep-focus lens that allows us to see it as an artefact of its own time that resonates in our own – can reveal much of our changing understandings of ourselves as social beings.

✕ Synopsis

American professor David Sumner (Dustin Hoffman) has left the US with his young wife Amy (Susan George) to spend a research sabbatical in the UK. They have come to a remote part of Cornwall, southwest England, settling at Trencher's Farm, Amy's former home. As the film opens, they are finishing a shopping trip to the local village, where they meet a number of the locals, including a former boyfriend of Amy's, Charlie Venner (Del Henney), and his uncle, the hard-drinking local patriarch Tom Hedden (Peter Vaughan). As David toils away at his mathematical research in the old family farmhouse, Amy becomes idle and bored, while outside a group of local men, including Venner, Chris Cawsey the rat-catcher (Jim Norton), and the surly, dangerous Norman Scutt (Ken Hutchison), work on repairing the garage roof. David, already covertly mocked by the workmen, continues to alienate himself from the community in an awkward encounter with a local magistrate, Major Scott (T. P. McKenna), the vicar Barney Hood (Colin Welland) and his wife Louise (Cherina Mann).

Unspoken hostilities fester, and the sexual tension rises between the possessive David, conflicted Amy and jealous locals: at one point, Amy strips to the waist at a landing window, in full view of the workmen. Soon afterwards, Amy's cat is strangled and hanged in the wardrobe; Amy tells David that either Scutt or Cawsey must have killed the animal 'to prove to you they could get into your bedroom', but David fails to confront them, much to Amy's chagrin. Instead, he attempts to ingratiate himself with them, accepting an invitation to join them for a snipe-hunting trip.

While David and the others are out on the moor, Venner returns to the house to find Amy alone. She invites him in and gives him a drink, apparently intent on asking him about the strangled cat. Venner makes a move to kiss her, she slaps him, and he strikes her; she falls to the floor, and he drags her to the sofa, where he forces himself upon her. However, what begins as rape seems to turn into consensual sex. Afterwards, as they are lying together, Scutt enters the house: he has followed Venner, and, unseen by Amy, he threatens his workmate with a shotgun. He then brutally rapes Amy while Venner holds her down.

Meanwhile, in a sequence Peckinpah intercuts with the rape scene, David has shot and killed a bird which he retrieves from the undergrowth only to return it to the bushes, shocked and saddened, rubbing his hands on his clothes in a vain attempt to clean off the blood. Finally realising he has been abandoned by the others, he returns from the hunting trip humiliated; Amy tells him nothing of what has happened to her. The next morning, David belatedly fires the workmen. That evening, the Sumners attend a church social, during which Amy struggles to maintain her composure, plagued by flashbacks to the rape. At the event, the mentally retarded Henry Niles (an uncredited David Warner) is lured away by a young villager, Janice Hedden (Sally Thomsett) (daughter of the patriarch Tom). In the awkward, tentative tryst that follows, Niles accidentally kills her. When she is noted as missing, and an initial search proves fruitless, a posse that includes Venner, Scutt, Cawsey and Tom Hedden attempts to find Niles. In the meantime, driving home through the fog, David and Amy have accidentally knocked down Henry Niles; they take the injured man back to the farm. When the villagers find out, they head out after him, fired up on whisky.

Venner, Scutt and Cawsey confront David and demand that he hands Niles over to them. David, sensing the situation is deteriorating into a potential lynching, refuses to comply. Major Scott arrives and attempts to defuse the situation, but the posse is now drunk and enraged by David's stubbornness. In a struggle over a shotgun, the Major is shot dead by Tom Hedden. Now realising that there is no way back, the men proceed to lay siege to the house, finally prompting David into violent, defensive and retaliatory action. At one point, Amy, at Venner's behest, attempts to let the men in, and she is brutally reprimanded by David. The violence that follows leaves all of the besiegers dead, with only David, Amy and Niles left standing. In the closing scene, David is driving Niles back to the village. When Niles says, 'I don't know my way home,' David replies, 'That's OK. I don't either.'

✖ Part 1

STRAW DOGS THEN

Genesis and Pre-Production

By the time *Straw Dogs* came into his sights, Peckinpah was riding high. *The Wild Bunch* (1969) had had limited box-office returns, due in part to a mishandled release strategy, but it had been hailed as a masterpiece by the most influential US critics, and its director seemed poised to reap the rewards of long years of hard work and perpetual disappointments. Some of the lustre may have been lost after the release of *The Ballad of Cable Hogue* in May 1970; its comic touches and lyrical tone had perplexed many reviewers, but it was never planned as a movie on the scale, or in the emotional register, of its predecessor. Expectations remained high for Peckinpah's next project.

At the start of the new decade, while completing *Cable Hogue*, Peckinpah had picked up on a script being developed from a British writer's potboiler novel, *The Siege of Trencher's Farm*, a violent, sensational tale of an American professor visiting rural England with his wife and young daughter, becoming embroiled in a blood-thirsty hunt for an escaped child killer. Gordon Williams's novel had been through another screenwriter's hands, but the results had disappointed Daniel Melnick, the producer who owned the screen rights. Melnick had produced Peckinpah's TV feature *Noon Wine* in 1966, and, having interested Peckinpah in the *Trencher's* project, and having piqued the curiosity of Martin Baum, President of ABC Pictures, Melnick commissioned a new screenplay from David Zelag Goodman. In Goodman's reworking, the American academic writing a critical study of an obscure eighteenth-century poet became, first, a lawyer and then a mathematics professor on sabbatical leave from the US, married to a young English woman, and returning with her to the village where she grew up (SPC Goodman, 1970a). An early draft retains the seven-year-old daughter Karen from the novel; the couple are named George and Louise Magruder, and

Louise is a Londoner, born and bred. Rewritten pages of the first draft, heavily annotated by Peckinpah, find Karen excised, the couple renamed David and Amy, David reimagined as a mathematician and Amy's close connection with the village established (SPC G&P, 1970b).

Further drafts included input from Melnick, Goodman and, chiefly, Peckinpah himself, usually working on his own. Hoffman also recalled spending some time on the script with Goodman, who in turn credits Hoffman with the fleshing out of David Sumner's character in particular; Goodman and Hoffman even visited a couple of universities as they worked on this aspect of the screenplay (Simmons, 1998, p. 125). Baum and Melnick were apparently both pleased with the version Peckinpah submitted in August 1970, although he continued to draft and redraft. In late 1970, he even sent a version to Harold Pinter, in the hope that the British playwright might be interested in having a go at it. Pinter had established himself as a screenwriter with some pedigree via successes such as *The Servant* (1963) and *The Quiller Memorandum* (1966), but he declined Peckinpah's offer, replying with poised politeness, while simultaneously dismissing the script as

> an abomination … obscene not only in its unequivocal delighted rape and violence but in its absolute lack of connection with anything that is recognisable or true in human beings and in its pathetic assumption that it is saying something 'important' about human beings. (SPC Pinter, 1970)

Peckinpah took this on the chin: 'Of course,' he shot back, 'but that's the point, isn't it? If it wasn't the joke would be too monstrous to behold' (SPC Peckinpah, 1970e). Having chalked up the skirmish with Pinter to experience – the story goes that Sam pinned Pinter's letter to a studio noticeboard (Pinter, 2001) – he persevered with the script, developing the relationships in particular, and the backstory for Amy and her ambivalent kind of homecoming.[3]

For many months, the film was referred to as *The Siege at Trencher's Farm*. Other potential titles included *The Square Root of Fear*, shot down by the director as 'bloody phucking [sic] awful' (SPC Peckinpah, 1970a). According to Marshall Fine, the eventual title derived from a chance meeting between Peckinpah and actor and writer Walter Kelly, whom the director befriended and invited to stay with him in London during pre-production (Fine, 2005, p. 195). Kelly quoted from the Chinese philosopher Lao Tzu an aphorism that has been rendered in several different forms, but which Peckinpah cited as follows:

> Heaven and Earth are ruthless and treat the myriad creatures as straw dogs. The sage is ruthless and treats the people like straw dogs ... Is not the space between Heaven and Earth like a bellows? (SPC Peckinpah, 1970d)

On 16 November, Peckinpah wrote to both Baum and Hoffman enclosing the quotation above, glossing it with the note:

> In the T'ien Yun in the Chang Tzu it is said that the straw dogs were treated with the greatest deference before they were used as an offering, only to be discarded and trampled upon as soon as they had served their purpose. (SPC Peckinpah, 1970d)

Baum was apparently nonplussed by Peckinpah's new title, but let it stand, for want of anything better (SPC Weitzner, 1971), and a memo from James Swann dated 6 January announced the title change to the crew (SPC Swann, 1971).

The casting of Dustin Hoffman had hung in the balance for some time. One amusing exchange of telegrams between producer and director finds the former confessing (or, presumably, jesting) that, 'I made a slight mistake[:] turns out Dustin wants to play Tom Hedden. What do you recommend? Love Dan'; to which Peckinpah succinctly replies, 'Commit suicide[.] S.P.' (SPC Melnick, 1970c and Peckinpah, 1970b). Others considered for the role included Beau Bridges (SPC Kavanagh, 1970), Elliott Gould, Donald

Sutherland, Stacy Keach, Anthony Hopkins (who turned it down) and Sidney Poitier. The latter apparently liked the script but did not think he was right for the role. A memo dated 22 December 1970 confirms Hoffman was in place by Christmas (along with Henney, Hutchison, McKenna and Vaughan) (SPC Anon, 1970b). However, casting Hoffman in the role of David Sumner had other implications, notably the raising of the budget from $1,070,221 to $2,117,263 and a corresponding rise in the studio's expectations of the film in financial terms (Weddle, 1996, p. 403). Hoffman's detailed and charismatic performances in *The Graduate* (1967) and *Midnight Cowboy* (1969) had garnered him two Oscar nominations, and it was clearly something of a coup to have him commit to the project.

After consideration of a number of high-profile candidates, including Diana Rigg, Hayley Mills, Jacqueline Bissett and Charlotte Rampling, and up-and-coming stars such as Judy Geeson, Pauline Collins and Carol White, the role of Amy went to the relatively unknown British actress Susan George, who was signed for the sum of $10,000 (Hoffman's fee was $600,000). However, Hoffman expressed reservations about the casting of his opposite number, fretting that the casting of such a young woman (she was twenty at the time, he thirty-four) lent the relationship between David and Amy a Lolita-ish tone, which he regarded as unhelpful (Simmons, 1998, p. 126).[4] Peckinpah, however, deflecting Hoffman's protests, was adamant that he would not do the movie without her. A supporting cast of British actors included veteran Peter Vaughan as Tom Hedden and David Warner as Henry Niles, although Warner's name would not appear in the credits. Over the years, this detail has spawned a number of conflicting stories. Warner, who had appeared in *The Ballad of Cable Hogue,* had broken both his feet during the shooting of a film in Italy and was recuperating when the call came from Peckinpah. According to Warner himself, rumour had it at the time that his accident had rendered him uninsurable, but he denies this categorically in an interview for a German DVD 2007 release of *Straw Dogs*. Warner claims that it was in fact an argument between his agent and ABC Pictures over the position of his name in the title credits that was the real issue; although it was clearly Hoffman and George's film, Warner was the most well-established star next to Hoffman himself, and his agent was apparently insisting on having his client's name above the title. According to Warner, he suggested to Peckinpah directly that he be removed from the credits entirely, and Peckinpah was predictably delighted by the two-fingered salute to convoluted film-business etiquette.[5]

Shooting and the Problem of Susan George

Accounts of the progress of the shoot vary, but it seems clear that all was not well in the early days of filming. Martin Baum flew to England at the request of Melnick, who indicated that both he and Hoffman were unimpressed by the rushes from the first few days' shooting (Simmons, 1998, p. 129). Baum was also dismayed by what he saw and, convinced that Peckinpah must be ill, had him checked over by a doctor, whereupon he was diagnosed with walking pneumonia and hospitalised in London. It seems that a night out drinking on the cliffs at Land's End with his new 'dog brother' Ken Hutchison (Scutt) may have been to blame.[6] In any case, the production, about halfway through its sixty-one-day schedule, was shut down for five days. If the disruption resulted in a degree of tension between director and star, it seems that there was also a good deal of mutual respect in their relationship. Peckinpah wrote to Baum that Hoffman was 'not only bright but takes a no with grace' (SPC Peckinpah, 1971b). Hoffman described Peckinpah to Garner Simmons as 'one of the few natural directors I've ever worked with'; Peckinpah, in turn, considered Hoffman 'sensational ... an incredible actor' (Simmons, 1998, pp. 132, 131). Accounts by both Simmons and Weddle include amusing anecdotes of horseplay, but at the same time a good deal of space was allowed for Hoffman's more Method-inspired strategies. One story from the set comes from the shooting of the first scene in the pub, and a close-up of Tom Hedden as he looks down at David's American sneakers. The moment was achieved, according to some reports, by Peckinpah ordering Dustin Hoffman to walk into the pub wearing no trousers, a stunt which provoked the desired response (a memo reveals that a reshoot was required for 'Hedden's POV of David's tennis shoes, insert, panning up' [SPC Anon, 1971d]). At the same time, Peckinpah's assistant Katy Haber remembers Hoffman being very absorbed in the development of his own character, and paying precise attention to props and costume.[7]

Peckinpah's drinking had been constant from the first day, his coffee laced with brandy and his fruit juice with vodka, according to Baum (Fine, 2005, p. 199). A memo from Peckinpah to Hutchison demanded that, 'When I drink on the set, you drink on the set[,] dog brother' (SPC Peckinpah, 1971c). On the same day, Peckinpah sent a string of twenty-four memos to cast and crew, increasingly unintelligible, often signed with false names and with notes for 'enc[losures]', including bottles of brandy for all and sundry, and one dozen roses for Susan George. When Peckinpah, somewhat recuperated, returned to Cornwall to complete the picture, work proceeded much more swiftly and productively, although a cable sent in March raised concerns about how much footage was being shot. Peckinpah, in a characteristically sarcastic retort, sent back a telex to Lew Rachmil, informing him: 'have cut the siege stop we have a better picture without it' (SPC Peckinpah, 1971e).[8] On the other hand, many of the cast members have commented in retrospect on Peckinpah's professionalism, the speed at which he set up and shot the scenes, and the excitement of working with him. Peter Vaughan also noted how tough the shoot was, in particular the siege sequence: 'We actually did break that farmhouse apart … it was an extremely violent couple of nights' work' (Weddle, 1996, p. 415).

That *Straw Dogs* was incubated in an environment dominated by machismo and male bonding – an environment mirroring the setting of the movie itself – should come as no surprise to anyone familiar with Peckinpah's work or his reputation. Stories that have filtered down over the years include tales of long nights in the pub where much of the film was shot, purportedly Actors Studio-style exercises in establishing characters and relationships, but which seem to have been more of an excuse for enthusiastic carousing than for serious research. While preparing to shoot *Straw Dogs*, Peckinpah had employed a new personal assistant, Katy Haber, whose first job had been to type up a draft of the screenplay. However, Haber was soon given an insight into the varied and unusual tasks she would have to undertake: Peckinpah had organised a dinner for the male cast members before leaving London for the Cornwall shoot, and gave Haber the task of arranging for prostitutes to be on hand at the party.[9] The actor T. P. McKenna, Haber remembers, was dancing on a pub table with a couple of prostitutes when he fell and fractured his arm – a story largely corroborated by Melnick.[10] McKenna spent the rest of the shoot with the arm in a sling, lending an appropriate subtext to the representation of his character, the broken arm of the law in a society that would rather police itself.

If the friction between Peckinpah and Hoffman sparked the star actor's performance in fruitful ways, the conflict between Peckinpah and Susan George was far more serious, complex and disturbing. A fuller discussion of the character of Amy follows in Part 3 (see pp. 86–98), but it is worth commenting at this point on the development (or deterioration) of the relationship between director and leading lady. George's own accounts of the process indicate that, while she and Hoffman built up a good rapport in early filming, his commitment to Method-acting techniques meant that his attitude towards her (as a person, not simply as a character) after the rape had been filmed was cold and dismissive. 'From a very kind and humorous and loving friendship, he had become extremely aloof', she told David Weddle. 'Mind games,' she explained; '... incredible mind games, coming from both Dustin and Sam' (Weddle, 1996, p. 424). Others were clearly shocked at the way Susan George was being treated by the director and star. The conflict over the filming of the rape scene is a particularly densely layered affair that is at times difficult to decipher. The precise order of events seems confused and different accounts contradict each other. Still, it is not difficult to detect a power game played out along gendered lines between this young, female, inexperienced actor and a group of older, more experienced men. The detailed analysis of the rape scene in Part 4 focuses specifically on the staging of the scene, and the way in which it was filmed and edited. Here, I intend to focus on the circumstances under which it was negotiated and set up. The parallels between Susan George's predicament and the ordeal her character experiences run alarmingly close.

Susan George was very young (only twenty) at the time she was cast in the role of Amy, her first major screen role, and it seems she was somewhat overwhelmed by the international movie scene. Peckinpah put her through a punishing schedule of interviews before casting her (George recalls at least six meetings before he announced she had won the part). The context for the negotiation over the rape scene at casting, however, is unclear. Although George recalls in interview that the script 'never went into specifics on paper' in terms of what would happen, what would be shot, and would not,[11] the shooting script seems to be, on the contrary, fairly detailed about what was intended. Whether or not a body double was employed is not quite clear. According to some accounts, Peckinpah refused George's requests for one to cover the nude scenes. However, a report in *Time* magazine claims that 'when Susan George balked at playing the rape scene all the way to the end, the director simply brought in a double and kept going' (SPC Cocks, 1971, p. 87). Peckinpah's assistant Katy Haber recalls body doubles being available on set, and remembers shooting second-unit footage for the rape scene without George's knowledge.[12] As they were unable to find a body double that matched Susan George exactly, two different doubles who matched Susan's contours were employed to film inserts of naked breasts and buttocks (Haber, 2009).[13]

When the time approached to film the rape scene, George became increasingly panicky. Dan Melnick encouraged her to confront Peckinpah directly, and she asked for him to write out exactly what he expected of her. When he refused, George, terrified of the rape scene and rapidly losing any sense of trust in her director, flatly refused to do the scene, putting herself in severe legal jeopardy, and threatening to sink her own acting career almost before it had started. A memo from Peckinpah to Melnick dated 15 March 1971 vents the director's fury at what he interprets as unacceptable behaviour:

I told you that she was becoming very bitchy about showing any part of her body, and that if she continued, we should be prepared to get a photographic double for the scene, otherwise we would go way beyond schedule, if we ever get the scene at all. I also thought your suggestion to discuss the matter with her agent and our lawyers was excellent, in the event of her refusal or stalling to be prepared to sue. You told me today that you had discussed the matter with her and let her feel that she would not have to do the rape scene. I repeat I was stunned.

Every effort should be made to have her make the rape, every effort should be made to let her know that if she holds us up, we are prepared to get a photographic double and file suit. If she is co-operative and is the fine actress I think she is, she will be it superbly well and this is the way I want it.

[...]

It is a very delicate scene to do and I must have her full co-operation, otherwise I feel a major re-write will be called for. (SPC Peckinpah, 1971d)

George was coaxed back to another negotiation with Peckinpah, during which he relented and gave a detailed account of what he wanted from what he apparently referred to as 'the best rape scene that's ever been shot'.[14] He told George that the scene would require nudity, that two men would assault her, and that, 'one is going to have sex with you, and the other man is going to bugger you' (Kermode, 2003, p. 9). According to Susan George herself, she told him that, on the basis of what he had asked, he should 'find [himself] another Amy'.[15] And she walked off the set.

We have no more detail on what Peckinpah told her. If anything was written down, those notes are not extant. However, there can be little doubt that he intended to shoot something explicit and graphic. Weddle reports that, when George was trying to persuade Peckinpah to tone it down, she was insistent that she could help him achieve what he intended 'without showing pubic hair' (Weddle, 1996, p. 422), which suggests that full frontal nudity was at least on the agenda. On the other hand, Peckinpah's memo to Melnick, quoted above, makes it clear (at least on this occasion) that he had

> no intention of coming anywhere near anything faintly smelling of pornogrophy [sic], I intend to shoot the scene as written. Pussies and penis' [sic] do not interest me. The emotional havoc that happens to Amy is the basis of our story. (SPC Peckinpah, 1971d)

At a time when such things were still almost entirely off limits in mainstream Hollywood film-making (see pp. 27–9), Susan George was understandably terrified. Her counter-proposal was that she would communicate what he wanted of her through her eyes – 'If you focus on my eyes and my body movements,' she told him, 'I promise you I will lead you down the road you wish to be led down. I will make you believe every bloody moment of it.' According to George, Peckinpah gave in, but (significantly) reserved the right to change his mind: 'Okay, I'll make a deal with you,' he said. 'I'll do it your way, and if, when we've done it your way, I'm not satisfied … then we have to do some things my way' (Weddle, 1996, p. 422).

In retrospect, it is tempting to read into all this some sub- or unconscious parallel between the narrative of the scene and the power game being played out between director and actor. George hints that Peckinpah was perturbed by her intelligence and that he saw the contest over the rape scene as some kind of a battle of wills. It is easy to admire her resistance to Peckinpah's demands. On the other hand, it is hard to know how much of Peckinpah's declared intentions was sheer bravado, since there were severe limitations on what he could have imagined getting past the censors (and Baum sent frequent reminders during shooting that he required an R-rated picture). Regrettably, but understandably, George's language in the Fremantle DVD release interview is of a piece with the male discourse. Again, she recognised the director's desire to film 'the best rape scene that had ever been shot' (George, 2002), a term that she uses several times, and which recurs in other biographies and oral accounts of this aspect of the shoot.[16] In her

attempt to persuade Peckinpah to drop his insistence on graphic nudity, Susan
George promised him that, 'If you let me do it my way, I can give you the most
provocative, beautiful, and telling rape scene you'll ever see!' (Weddle, 1996,
p. 422). Again, these terms are disturbing – how can a rape scene be
'beautiful'? In what sense 'provocative'? – although she also claims to have told
him that she would help him achieve what he wanted, '... but on my terms',[17]
thereby (at least trying to) insist upon some sense of agency in the process. 'He
knew I was smart and a thinker,' she told Weddle.

> [A]nd he knew I was wicked, and all of it was attractive to him, and yet
> he would have loved to rip it all away from me so that I would have to go
> and claim it back. (Weddle, 1996, p. 411)

The description of Peckinpah's desire to 'rip' these qualities away from her –
qualities that resisted his attempt to assert his authority – and her
corresponding submissiveness ('so that I would have to go and claim it back')
are in keeping with her other references to their negotiations, and are oddly
reminiscent of the emotional and psychological assault Amy endures.[18]
Elsewhere, too, uncomfortable overtones of the David/Amy/Charlie triangle
can be detected in the way she speaks about working with her director: 'Sam
was so volatile and lethal on the one hand, and so quiet and kind and loving on
the other, that's what was fascinating about him' (Weddle, 1996, p. 423).

As work on the scene began, Susan George found herself undermined
by Peckinpah's refusal to engage with her: 'he never moved and he never said a
word to me for five days,' she told Weddle, only occasionally smiling at her.
Meanwhile, Del Henney was on the receiving end of a different kind of abuse.
Reports suggest that Henney hated the scene, and had great difficulty playing
it. 'Harrowing' is how he described it to Weddle, and Peckinpah reputedly
mocked him for his reluctance (Weddle, 1996, p. 423). Having conceded some
ground to Susan George, Peckinpah may have found a way to retaliate by
taunting her during the filming of the rape sequence, ostensibly to coax a
stronger performance from her: 'Wait till your parents get a load of this rape

scene we're gonna shoot, baby,' he told her at one point. 'How do you think they're gonna react, think they'll be proud of their precious girl then?' (Weddle, 1996, p. 419). Katy Haber also recalls Peckinpah taking his lead actress aside just before shooting the church social scene, telling her that her father was old and sick and may not live to see the finished film, then calling for 'action' as George began to well up.

Dan Melnick and Katy Haber have both spoken in quite strong terms about how shocked they were by the way Peckinpah (and Hoffman, too) treated Susan George during the latter stages of the production. Haber's perspective on Sam's behaviour is that it was about pragmatism; she sees it not as a power struggle *per se,* but as a strategy on the director's part. The focus was always, relentlessly upon what was necessary for the movie. According to Katy Haber, 'Sam just wanted to get the best performance he could get from Susan and he got it. Even if it meant putting her through some of the most important changes in her professional career' (Haber, 2009). Susan George herself is, in retrospect, remarkably forgiving of both Peckinpah and Hoffman, reasoning that 'that's the way they worked, and I believe to this day and always will that Peckinpah was a genius, likewise Hoffman, so I was willing to take anything and everything they had to give' (Weddle, 1996, p. 424). She apparently remains convinced that what Peckinpah ended up printing for the final cut of the movie had been in line with her request: 'And he did what I begged him to do, which was focus on my eyes and upper body and let me tell the story,' she told David Weddle.[19] Whether or not this round can be chalked up as a victory for Susan George, after a gruelling week of filming, she found herself unceremoniously shut out of the screening of the rushes, leaving her to fret over her performance. Thrown into fear and self-doubt again, she spent the time wondering 'whether I'd managed to pull it off or not, and just how angry he was going to be if I hadn't' (Weddle, 1996, p. 423). Finally Peckinpah emerged, walked towards her stony faced, and then held out a hand to her: 'You got it,' he told her, according to the 2002 interview, a greeting for which she was presumably meant to feel deeply grateful.

Sarah Projansky sees the 'sheer number of representations of rape that have appeared on screen since the 1970s' as 'a sustained definition of women as sexually victimized and a sustained cultural assault on women' (Projansky, 2001, p. 95). Debates about Peckinpah's own misogyny – the extent to which it impacted on his representations of women in his films, and arguments over whether it is just to brand him a misogynist in the first place – are only marginally relevant in this regard, and betray a failure to historicise *Straw Dogs* adequately. The rape scene in *Straw Dogs* exists within a tightly controlled male environment: written by men, enforced on a reluctant young actress isolated and in fear of Peckinpah's capacity for humiliating and intimidating his actors, and filmed, I will argue, in a way that runs the risk of eroticising the sexual assault. Weddle's description of the scene as 'one of the most perversely erotic sequences in cinema history' (1996, p. 424), consciously or not, cuts to the heart of the matter; in a Hollywood that (still) demands that its stars meet certain standards of conventional beauty, and that they obediently parade it for their audiences, the rape of Amy on screen, and the ordeal Susan George endured behind the scenes, is one of the clearest illustrations of the dominant, persistent, controlling male hand over the industry.

The Editing Process; Shaping an Ending

After the rape scene, it was probably the film's conclusion that caused the most heated debate during shooting. Early drafts had David driving away from the house and, immediately afterwards, Bertie (Michael Mundell), Bobby Hedden (Len Jones) and 'four teenagers' entering to confront Amy; the screenplay ends with Amy standing with a poker 'half raised in her hand ... her face twisting'. She has one enigmatic final line ('Of course!') and the movie ends with a freeze frame (SPC G&P, 1970c, p. 155). The second draft, corrected screenplay, a month later, pits Amy and David together against the village teenagers, both of them grinning, David armed with a poker and Amy with a knife (SPC G&P, 1970e, p. 140). A later revision has their assailants 'armed with sticks and clubs' (SPC G&P, 1971a, p. 147). By 8 April, just a few days before the production wrapped, the variations seem to have been whittled down to three possibilities. A memo from Melnick reads:

> It would be very helpful if you would dictate a short note describing the way you see the three endings which we have been discussing, i.e.:
> 1   Amy and David together (emotionally, if not necessarily physically) after the carnage
> 2   Bobby Hedden and kids entering after Siege and menacing David and Amy
> 3   (which I guess is an extension of 1) David ultimately leaving Amy alone and walking out the door 'ambiguously'
> As discussed, I will then attempt to get approval to shoot all three with the understanding that we will give each one 'its best shot'.
>
> (SPC Melnick, 1971b)

According to a memo from director to producer, Hoffman 'flatly refuse[d] to shoot the so-called happy ending ... after we started shooting in Cornwall' (SPC Peckinpah, 1971f). What emerged was something else again; while Peckinpah favoured the downbeat, second ending – one that would have circled neatly back to the opening title sequence, with its eerie shots of children playing in a graveyard, the studio favoured a more positive and less ambiguous denouement. The final ending, confirmed by 22 April at the latest (SPC Swann, 1971), seems to have derived from an improvisation between Hoffman and Warner. Henry Niles's dazed line, 'I don't know my way home' is answered by Sumner's 'That's OK. I don't either,' a succinct expression of the devastating transformation David has undergone (the original cut of this final scene included a much longer dialogue between the two characters [Rachmil, 1971d, p. 9]). Although David and Amy have survived, the fact that he leaves her alone in the house at the end, coupled with his rueful final line, means that the movie is much more likely to leave its viewers unsettled than it is to leave them reassured.

By the time the editing process began, Peckinpah was already in Arizona preparing for his next picture, *Junior Bonner* (1972). It was decided that Melnick and Roger Spottiswoode, assisted by Bob Wolfe (who had worked on *The Wild Bunch*) would edit, guided by regular, usually weekly meetings and screenings with Peckinpah. From these sessions, the director's extensive notes would steer the next stage in the process. According to Marshall Fine, the siege sequence was cut from 100 minutes of footage, to thirty, and finally to eighteen minutes (2005, p. 207). In the editing process, some of the more graphically violent shots seem to have been dropped: at one point, ABC production supervisor Lewis Rachmil expressed relief at deletion of what he referred to as the cheek-biting scene, 'particularly in view of our discussions relative to the amount of violence and its cumulative effect' (SPC Rachmil, 1971b).

However, ABC's chief preoccupation remained the issue of sexuality in general, and the rape scene in particular. Amongst the notes on the script from producer to director in July 1970 is Melnick's objection to a suggestion of incestuous sexual foreplay between Bobby and Janice Hedden, passing on a request from Martin Baum to 'Please eliminate "budding nipple" manipulations.' He added: '[Baum] accepts the fact that this will be an R-rated film, but "for God's sakes not an X"' (SPC Melnick, 1970b, p. 6). In January 1971, another memo from Melnick to Peckinpah states that Baum has asked that they keep in mind 'his strong conviction that American audiences are now rejecting films with "foul language and unnecessary indecent exposure"' (SPC Melnick, 1971a). In April, a memo from Rachmil to Peckinpah and Melnick included copies of an article from the *New York Times,* added in order 'to re-inforce his [Baum's] caution that he realizes the picture will get an "R" rating … but that it be an easy "R" and not one that could turn into an "X"' (SPC Rachmil, 1971a); the article claimed that a number of film companies have put 'an outright ban on X-category films', and 'have also decided to make very few, if any, R-category films' (Phillips, 1971, p. 1).

As early as July 1970, in fact, Peckinpah's approach to the rape scene was being queried as Baum and Melnick fretted over the draft screenplays. Jottings from one meeting with Melnick include the note, 'For M. B. [Marty

Baum] clean up rape scene' (SPC Anon, 1970a). Melnick insisted that, 'Amy ultimately makes it with Venner out of her anger with David and the desire to possess and dominate someone who "looks up to her".' He questioned the scene's conclusion in early drafts, which had Amy putting Scutt and Venner down by 'asking for more', and was adamant that 'she should not abandon herself wantonly to Scutt's rape' (SPC Melnick, 1970a). Goodman, though he told Peckinpah he thought the rape scene was a stroke of genius, agreed with Melnick (SPC Goodman, 1970b, p. 3). Certainly by the time the shooting script was finalised, Amy's complex response to the rape had been adjusted; what starts as assault would turn into love-making between her and Venner, and this would be set against the violent rape at the hands of Scutt. Her taunting and retaliatory dialogue, included in earlier drafts, was excised.

What was in the script was one thing. However, as Susan George herself had discovered, there was always the potential for significant differences, and more intractable problems, when the script was taken from the page, into action, and onto celluloid. A rough cut of the rape scene (and some of the siege sequence) had left a room full of ABC executives very shaken up. With the threat of an 'X' certificate growing, Lew Rachmil wrote to Peckinpah:

> The entire sequence is just TOO MUCH of everything. It is excessive and as a result becomes ordinary and vulgar. As cut it destroys the ambivalence in Amy's problem of wanting Venner and then not wanting him and finally winding up in disgust.
>
> There is <u>too much</u> explicit pornography – the pushing, grunting, paying [sic] with nipples. ... <u>Too much</u> is played in long shots or medium long shots thus revealing more of the sexual activity. There is <u>too much</u> slapping of Amy in the beginning.

He goes on to suggest that the second rape could be excised completely and concludes: 'As I pointed out in the projection room, ABC has the final editing position and will use it should it not see the sequence done in your "good taste and better judgement"'(SPC Rachmil, 1971c). His next communication is more concessionary, although he still complains that there is 'too much moving, grinding and moaning after the line "Easy"'(SPC Rachmil, 1971d).

Although it is unclear what was cut before submission to the censorship and certification boards on each side of the Atlantic, and what was cut subsequently, it would seem that the entire scene ended up being more condensed than it appears to be in the shooting script, and, in all likelihood, in an initial rough cut screened for Melnick, Rachmil and others. It would seem that the original intention was to include a longer, more tender love-making scene between Amy and Charlie that would more clearly demarcate the initial assault from the consensual sex that follows. This would then be brutally disrupted by the arrival of Scutt. With details of editing apparently resolved between ABC staff and Peckinpah and his team, the next hurdle to be negotiated would be the certification process. To grasp fully the nuances of the negotiations between production company and the MPAA and BBFC that would follow, it is important to understand the wider cultural context for the reception of such a challenging film.

England Swings, America Rocks: *Straw Dogs* in Its Cultural Context

Although there is insufficient space here to provide an in-depth study either of the counterculture movement in the US in the late 1960s, of the rise of feminism during the same period, or of the beginning of a conservative backlash in the early 1970s, these cultural currents are highly significant in an appraisal of *Straw Dogs* in its context. They facilitate a fuller understanding both of the world of the film itself – David and Amy's backstory, David's pacifism and its violent reversal – and of the context in which the film was made and subsequently received by audiences and critics. The movie stirred up trouble on both sides of the Atlantic, stepping as it did into the middle of a pitched battle between forces of liberalism, intent on reducing censorship, and a rising tide of moral conservatism that was deeply disturbed by what it saw as a breakdown in acceptable standards of social and particularly sexual behaviour. In addition, the problematic character of Amy and her brutal treatment at the hands of the male characters in the film, complicated the controversies over screen violence still further, with feminist protests (which seemed to share some common ground with both liberals and conservatives) adding to the furore that threatened to engulf the movie's first appearance before a paying audience. Some thirteen years later, it would be caught in another wave of moral panic in the so-called 'video-nasty' era in Britain in the mid-1980s.

The conditions that took *Straw Dogs* and turned it into a bloody bone for a number of different factions to fight over for many years are complex. At the heart of the controversy are a couple of taboos that Peckinpah's movie confronts head on; by crossing the live wires of sex and violence, he ignited a debate that still rages forty years later. However, to appreciate fully the impact of *Straw Dogs* upon the culture in 1971, it is necessary to understand the state of censorship in the UK and US at that time, and the wider cultural lie of the land that gave rise to the increasingly uneasy relationship between film-makers and certification bodies. Contemporary attitudes towards sex and violence on screen, in particular, were shaped by a social revolution that redrew the map in terms of gender and sexuality, relations between citizens and the state, and by a startling rise in crime and public displays of violence in the United States.

In his part-memoir, part-social history of the era, Todd Gitlin discusses the 'Gathering of the Tribes' spectacle at Golden Gate Park in 1968. His account is tempered by the jaded eye of hindsight, as he describes how, 'twenty thousand people, more or less, revelled, dropped acid, burned incense, tootled flutes, jingled tambourines, passed out flowers, admired one another, felt the immensity of their collective spectacle' (Gitlin, 1993, p. 210). The cultural dissidence of Gitlin's generation took on a dizzying array of forms across the spectrum, with hippies 'dropping out' at one end, and radicals marching in their thousands at the other. Gitlin himself was a student at the University of California, Berkeley where, a few years earlier, the Berkeley Free Speech Movement had been established. It was the first of many such politicised student groups that would spring up around the country, providing, amongst other things, a solid base for protests against the Vietnam War as the draft expanded, more coffins were flown home, and disillusionment grew deeper and more widespread amongst the American people, especially the youth, vulnerable to the draft. Furthermore, links between the Berkeley undergraduate population and the 'hippy' set centred in Haight-Ashbury were strong, if mutually suspicious, with student radicalism occasionally rubbing uneasily against a spirit of 'turn on, tune in, drop-out'.

David Zelag Goodman, working on a screen adaptation of the very British thriller *The Siege of Trencher's Farm* (1969) by Scottish writer Gordon Williams, was aware of these cultural shifts, and in an interview for the UK TV documentary *Man Trap* (Channel 4, 2003), made direct reference to the Vietnam War. Indeed, the finished film is far more incisive in its analysis of turn-of-the-decade American culture than it is of rural English life, even if the scorn the British reviewers poured upon its depiction of Cornish villagers was probably unjustified. An early draft mentions that Sumner's professional background is in an academic post at Berkeley – that crucible of student activism (SPC G&P, 1970c, p. 19A). Furthermore, we find in Goodman's first draft of the screenplay a series of references to a court case that were excised early on during the collaboration with Peckinpah, but which Goodman had initially set great store by, noting that they should be 'SIMPLY AND CLEARLY DRAMATIZING for us on the SCREEN ... one CRUCIAL ASPECT of our HERO'S CURRENT STATE OF MIND'. In four scenes interspersed through the main plot, George/David recalls appearing as one of the defence lawyers for four 'young yippys [sic]' (SPC Goodman, 1970a, p. 6).

Spearheaded by Abbie Hoffman and Jerry Rubin, the Youth International Party was a high-profile group of activist pranksters. It made its most audacious assault on the establishment in August 1968, targeting the Democratic Convention in Chicago, where the Party was due to select its candidate for the election later that year. The demonstration was trailed for months with incendiary publicity, countered by Chicago Mayor Richard Daley's vociferous threats about maintaining law and order. With the yippy consensus splintering, Abbie Hoffman's dream of half a million attending his 'Festival of Life' flickered and all but died. The few thousand youths who did attend a series of protests and events were met with strong-arm tactics by the police and the National Guard. Several days of violent clashes ensued; a grandly planned, star-studded concert eventually featured just one long set by the MC5, interrupted by the approach of a police baton charge (at the sight of which the band members headed for the hills). However, the real drama played out in the court case that followed, and this is where the link with the development of the *Straw Dogs* script becomes clear: eight men, including Hoffman and Rubin, were charged with conspiracy to incite a riot. The trial, presided over by a judge who made no attempt to maintain neutrality, frequently deteriorated into absurdist theatre, with witnesses such as Judy Collins and a stoned Country Joe McDonald bursting into song from the witness box, to the horror of the court officials. More disturbingly, defendant (and Black Panther leader) Bobby Seale was handcuffed and gagged in the courtroom after interrupting proceedings, and given a four-year prison sentence for contempt of court (Doggett, 2007, pp. 293–301). Five of the other defendants were found guilty and sentenced, but allowed out on bail within a fortnight; in 1972, all the convictions were overturned.

This case, variously known today as the Trial of the Chicago Eight, or the Chicago Seven, or the Chicago Conspiracy, crystallises much of what was at stake around the time the *Straw Dogs* project was in development. It is probable that the trial itself provided the inspiration for the series of flashbacks Goodman had written into the first draft of his script. Reports from the Chicago trial detail shouting matches between the judge, attorneys and defendants, and in Goodman's third flashback sequence, all the lawyers, save George, are on their feet shouting at the judge (p. 51). In the final flashback,

THE SCREEN FREEZES ON THIS FRAME OF THE SHOUTING DEFENCE LAWYER UNABLE
TO BELIEVE THAT GEORGE HAS SAID NOR DONE ANYTHING ... AND GEORGE
TURNING AWAY FROM THE DEFENCE LAWYER'S LOOK. (SPC Goodman, 1970a,
p. 57)

By the time of the second draft, this device had completely disappeared;
George Magruder, the lawyer writing a book about Civil Rights, became
David Sumner the 'astro-mathematician' and the flashbacks were replaced by
moments of tension and dispute between David and Amy over his decision to
flee America for England because 'there was no place left to hide'. Admittedly
the original device is clumsy, and David's turn from pacifism to violent
retaliation is expressed in a far more sophisticated manner in the finished film.
Nevertheless, it illustrates how the film was from the outset sensitive to the
conflict and unrest of the times. Hoffman clearly saw his character as a man
'fleeing the violent campus situation in America for the peaceful English
countryside' (Simmons, 1998, p. 126). David may have outrun the violence of
his own country, possibly even the draft but the distant thunder of a society at
war with itself is never out of earshot.

Feminism and the Sexual Revolution

Retrospective analysis of America in the 1960s generally falls into two camps
– the relieved and the regretful. Right-wing commentators see the failure of
the counterculture to achieve any real, substantial political change as a narrow
escape for civilisation. For the left, it was a fleeting opportunity tragically
squandered. The Civil Rights movement made great strides forward, but even
over forty years later, in an era when a black man can become President of the
United States, racism remains embedded in social structures and in living
communities across the US. American foreign policy looks as misguided as
ever in the wake of failures in Afghanistan and Iraq and the rollercoaster of
capitalism is screaming its way through another lurching downturn. It could

be argued that the most complete revolution of the period was, in fact, the sexual one. The approval of the birth-control pill by the Federal Drug Administration in the US in 1960 allowed women for the first time a degree of sexual freedom and autonomy previously undreamt of. By 1965, almost 6 million American women were on the pill (Ehrenreich *et al.*, 1986, p. 42). In 1966, William Masters and Virginia Johnson published *Human Sexual Response*, an exhaustive study (including observation and filmed record of some 10,000 male and female orgasms) that revealed how wide the gap had been between the public discourse and private sexual practice of the American people. The revolution in sexual behaviour and changing attitudes towards sexuality opened up possibly the biggest generational rift of the period. By the late 1960s and early 70s, there was no stopping the rising tide of what the establishment called permissiveness, and what the majority of young people called freedom.

It may be difficult for anyone who did not live through it to grasp fully the impact feminism had on US culture at this time. Today the movement tends to be most evident and active in the academy. However, in the 60s and 70s, it was both a very vocal and a very practical initiative, overseeing amongst other things the establishment of health clinics, rape crisis centres and abortion-referral services in major urban centres across the US. Women's roles in society were being reappraised in unprecedented ways. Betty Friedan's bestselling *The Feminine Mystique* (1963) laid down an early challenge to the contented, affluent, settled domesticity that had been seen as the appropriate niche for American women in the post-war consumerist boom. However, it was not until the beginning of the 1970s that women's liberation started to become a powerful social revolutionary force. The National Organization of Women (NOW) had been established in 1966, with landmark events including the picketing of the Miss America beauty pageant in 1968, where they crowned a live sheep to mimic the way women were 'appraised and judged like animals at a county fair' (Echols, 1994, p. 149); they also staged a display of binning bras, girdles and other symbols of their oppression.[20]

In the more rarefied atmosphere of the academy, Kate Millett's *Sexual Politics*, Shulamith Firestone's *The Dialectic of Sex* and Germaine Greer's *The Female Eunuch* were all published close together around the turn of the decade, and while there was inevitably a gulf between the academy and mainstream culture, there were also moments when the gap was bridged. On 26 March 1970, the feminist activist Susan Brownmiller confronted *Playboy* founder Hugh Hefner on *The Dick Cavett Show* (1968–74), suggesting that women would achieve equality on the day Hefner was willing to appear on TV with a cottontail attached to his rear end. April 1971 saw a public showdown featuring Greer, new NOW president Jacqueline Ceballos and lesbian feminist Jill Johnston on one rampart and Norman Mailer on the other; Mailer had recently published his own response to the women's liberation movement, *The Prisoner of Sex,* and the event held at New York City's town hall was a night of fierce, theatrical debate (captured on film by Chris Regedus and D. A. Pennebaker in their fascinating 1979 documentary *Bloody Town Hall*). The film illustrates not only the sense of bewilderment felt by many men in the face of a growing challenge to the patriarchal establishment, but also the deep rifts within feminism itself – from the liberal wing represented by literary critic Diana Trilling, to the more militant Greer, to the radical Johnston, who insisted that lesbianism had to be an integral part of the feminist agenda, and who rejected heterosexuality and monogamy as inevitable corollaries of a patriarchal system.

The mismatch between the counterculture's sexual mores – sexual disinhibition and experimentation that centred mainly around the male sexual ego – and the feminist agenda, which demanded a reappraisal of relations between men and women, including the realm of sexuality – sparked one of our most enduring cultural conundrums: how can a woman establish an autonomous heterosexual identity free of male requirement, expectation or prejudice? Even in the hippy ethos of free love, the sexual revolution had been predominately male-oriented, and the alternative lifestyle did not embrace any kind of reappraisal of gender roles. As Mark Donnelly puts it, 'Feminists … saw that the narrative of the counter-culture was male-dominated and that its ideal of "sexual liberation" was typically defined on men's terms' (2005,

p. 130). In the UK, the emergence of a feminist agenda was a longer time coming, and dismissive attitudes, condemning feminists as extremist, or even old-fashioned (via an historical link back to bluestockings and suffragettes), prevailed. A demonstration at the 1970 Miss World contest, where Bob Hope was pelted with smoke bombs and flour, mirrored the US event two years earlier, and certainly brought considerable press attention. On the other hand, the patronising, dismissive attitude that was the most common response is neatly summed up by Prince Charles – twenty-two years' old at the time – who reflected that, 'Basically, I think it is because they want to be men' (cited in Sandbrook, 2006, p. 664).

When, in the opening moments of *Straw Dogs*, the camera's gaze is entranced by the sight of a braless Amy strolling down the village street, when David and Amy argue later over her provocative dress sense, the film, consciously or not, is taking a vivid snapshot of contemporary sexual mores. The feminist Robin Morgan's famous slogan, 'Pornography is the theory; rape is the practice' (1974, p. 139), repeatedly invoked by pro-censorship feminists, takes on an interesting complexion when considered in relation to the film, and the 'Problem of Amy' section explores this further (see pp. 86–98). Issues of sexual possession and domination, so crucial in the film, need to be understood within a cultural context that was deeply conflicted: on the one hand, a greater degree of sexual freedom was being grasped as a right; on the other, the precise impact such a monumental change was having on relations between men and women was hard to determine, and the cause of profound unease on the part of those seeking to challenge the sexism that remained engrained even in the most revolutionary political movements of the era.

Backlash: Morality, Censorship and the MPAA

As dramatic as the counterculture's arrival had been, the splintering of consensus and collapse of utopian aspirations, to be replaced by an inward gaze and a woozy kind of hedonism, was just as rapid, and the first years of the

However, the shifts in the MPAA's procedures were generating wider ripples in the culture of the time, particularly amongst younger, hipper journalists. In July 1971, around the time that Dr Aaron Stern was appointed Head of CARA, Jack Valenti had published a short essay in *Harper's Bazaar* with the forthright title 'In Defense of the Voluntary Film Rating Program'. The essay was intended to answer critics who felt that the MPAA was not doing enough to stem the tide of permissiveness; a couple of months earlier, the National Catholic Office for Motion Pictures (formerly the National Legion of Decency) had sent up a flare by withdrawing its support for the ratings system. Valenti insisted that the MPAA sought only to make a judgement on the 'suitability of the viewing of [a] movie by young people'; it was not the job of the rating programme to recommend, ban or censor movies (SPC Valenti, 1971). In October, Peckinpah received an invitation to participate in a Filmex sponsored panel discussion, 'Artistic Freedom: Restraints and Responsibilities', at LA County Museum planned for 9 November. Beverly Walker, one of the organisers of the discussion, mentioned in her letter to the director that she had heard that *Straw Dogs* had been given an 'X', and that ABC was insisting on an 'R'-rated cut. 'This is disgusting,' she wrote. 'It is appalling how little courage so many people in the industry have shown in revolting against this man [Aaron Stern].' She concluded: 'We hope our panel will be hot and controversial, and bring out in the open the issues' (SPC Walker, 1971). A leaflet in the Peckinpah Collection outlines the panel discussion, suggesting that the organisers had a very firm grasp on the issues that were troubling the MPAA and the studios at this juncture, in particular debates about whether film-makers should have the same freedom as other artists, or whether 'working in a mass medium places special responsibility upon the artist'; and asking, 'with radically changing social and sexual attitudes, what is the role of film in exploring important new concepts of sexual relationships and sexual identity?' (SPC Anon, 1971e).

    Also slated to appear on the panel was Stephen Farber, who had recently completed a stint working on a fellowship programme set up by the MPAA itself, aimed at allowing young people greater access to the

Association's working practices. Farber and another intern, Estelle Changas, had written a piece for the *Los Angeles Times* that was highly critical of the MPAA's policies and working practices. Presumably as a result of the controversy stirred up by their *Times* article, Aaron Stern refused to appear on a panel with Farber, who was forced to step down. By Farber's account, the conference was a lively event, perhaps even more 'hot and controversial' than Beverly Walker had anticipated in her letter to Peckinpah, and several vociferous members of the audience insisted that Farber be allowed up on stage, which he was, albeit briefly. However, Peckinpah seemed to have adopted a stance that would set the pattern for forthcoming exchanges in the press. Farber recalls that 'Sam seemed somewhat ill at ease in the role of apologist for censorship', and remained fairly quiet. It was left to another panellist, Yugoslavian director Dusan Makavejev, writer and director of the sexually explicit *WR: Mysteries of the Organism* (1971), to attack Stern's position (Farber, 2009).

A few short months later, in April 1972, Changas and Farber's essay 'Putting the Hex on "R" and "X"' was republished in the *New York Times*. According to their research, the MPAA's level of involvement was far greater than Valenti's *Harper's* piece had suggested. Drawing on their own experience as interns at the MPAA, they pointed out that scripts were routinely submitted and sent back with strong recommendations on deletions and editing. Their conclusion was radical, casting doubt upon the idea of a director's vision and autonomy: 'Films are emasculated before shooting even begins,' they argued (SPC Farber and Changas, 1972, p. 1). Citing the role of Stern in the process, they singled out a number of films that had been subjected to this kind of treatment, but reserved detailed discussion for Peckinpah's *Straw Dogs,* which they noted had originally been rated 'X' by CARA, and had eventually been awarded an 'R' certificate after heavy editing.

The *Times* article would provoke a series of letters from directors, as well as Stern, in the days that followed. When the controversy broke, Peckinpah was courted by Stern, who was keen to enlist the support of

Hollywood directors in answering the charges laid against the MPAA and CARA. Enclosing copies of supportive replies from directors Don Siegel (*Dirty Harry*, 1971) and Ernest Lehman (*Portnoy's Complaint*, 1972), Stern insisted that Peckinpah's response was 'crucial to me because of the prolonged reference to STRAW DOGS'. He signed off in anticipation of Peckinpah's backing, writing, 'I really appreciate your help, Sam, and look forward to seeing you and Joey soon. Deep Affection, Aaron' (SPC Stern, 1972). Peckinpah's letter to the *Times* is fascinating for the way it does not simply sit on the fence, but rather performs some kind of frantic dance around it. Typically acerbic, Peckinpah blusters, 'I detest censorship in any form' but concedes that, 'like subsidies, suppositories, taxes and the Nixon Administration, it seems to be part of the American way of life, and has to be dealt with' (SPC Peckinpah, 1972b). He cedes more ground when he insists upon expressing his 'appreciation of the extraordinary cooperation of Dr. Aaron Stern, who bent over backwards to keep the intent of "Straw Dogs" intact'. Of course, the letter flatly contradicts Peckinpah's comments elsewhere: In December 1971, he had been quoted as complaining that 'the cuts strike out "35 per cent of the effectiveness" of one of the two main scenes' – i.e. the rape scene (SPC Blevins, 1971). For Farber and Changas, the censoring of the film had had a much more severe impact. In remarkably prescient analysis that pre-empts much of the controversy that has lingered ever since, they write:

> Peckinpah's original version meant to contrast Susan George's responses to the rapes – the second rape was as frightening and revolting as the first was erotic; the scene, as originally shot, implicated us and made us confront our own ambivalent responses to violence. Interestingly, it was the rating board, not Sam Peckinpah, that was responsible for reinforcing a sexist fantasy. In shearing the scene the board said, in effect: a rape enjoyed by a woman can be seen by children, but a rape that truly violates and humiliates her cannot appear on the screen. (SPC Farber and Changas, 1972, p. 15)[22]

Farber was clearly disappointed with Peckinpah's failure to take a stand, as a series of letters that followed between him and the director indicates. Another notable critic of the MPAA, Vincent Canby, publicly took Peckinpah to task for his timidity, writing in the *New York Times* soon after:

> I couldn't care less whether someone of the stature of Sam Peckinpah thinks that Dr. Stern's advice made, say, 'Straw Dogs' a better film. ... It's very depressing to hear him, of all people, carrying on in praise of public moralists who spend their days measuring frames of pubic hair, counting four-letter words and trying to figure out whether a certain sex act indicates sodomy or is just a variation on the conventional frontal approach. (SPC Canby 1972b, p. 18)

I will return to this issue in the detailed discussion of the rape scene (see pp. 101–15). For now, it is sufficient to note that, as so often in such cases, those who wielded the scissors, intent on a moral clean-up campaign, committed instead an act of vandalism that defaced the film, and rendered its more complex subtext unintelligible.

Straw Dogs, American Audiences and American Critics

As the next section will show, critics in the UK were almost unanimous in their condemnation of *Straw Dogs*. The US critics were generally far more positive, particularly in their response to the film's representation of violence. Some accounts, however, suggest that the previews were stormy: according to David Weddle's biography, the first public showing took place at the North Point Theater, San Francisco, and a third of the audience walked out of the packed auditorium before the end, 'yelling comments like, "This is obscene!" as they marched up the aisles' (Weddle, 1996, pp. 425–6). Weddle also records a story told by Melnick that has Peckinpah being literally chased from the cinema by an enraged member of the audience; Melnick recalls his shock at hearing rows of people cheering Sumner on through the carnage of the film's climax.

One of the most difficult factors in piecing together a more detailed picture of the early reception of *Straw Dogs*, however, is uncovering the audience demographic. A survey commissioned by the MPAA in 1968 reveals that the 16–24 age group accounted for 48 per cent of box-office admissions that year (Cook, 2000, p. 67). An article published in *Variety* in the same year proclaimed that 'Being young and single is the overriding demographic pre-condition for being a frequent and enthusiastic moviegoer' (cited in Maltby, 2003, p. 173). David Cook notes the box-office success of a number of youth-oriented films at this time such as *The Graduate* (starring Dustin Hoffman) and *Bonnie and Clyde*; the former would turn out to be the highest-grossing film of the decade. Cook also cites several Hollywood studio executives' public acknowledgement of the need to 'keep up with the rhythm of young people', in the words of one Twentieth Century-Fox vice-president (2000, p. 68). The shift goes a long way towards explaining the rise of the American auteur directors, including Roman Polanski, Arthur Penn, Martin Scorsese and Peckinpah himself, making films for a more cine-literate generation seeking movies more attuned to their own preoccupations and values. The same impetus was responsible for the birth of the youth cult movie typified by *Easy Rider* (1969), as executives realised that substantial box-office returns could be secured for a relatively small outlay. Cook suggests that the primary audience for *The Wild Bunch*, with 'its R-rated violence[,] was in the 17–25-year-old age group' too (p. 82), and one would presume that the same would have applied to *Straw Dogs*. Certainly the publicity machine used controversy over the film's violence as grist to its mill, featuring striking images such as a close-up of Hoffman with one shattered lens in his spectacles shedding splinters of glass across his face (see over). At the same time, taglines emphasised the film's body count ('The knock at the door meant the birth of one man and the death of seven others!') at the expense of its more reflective meditation on violence and pacifism, as did the publicity blurb worked up for the release:

Before long the couple discovers that beneath the peaceful façade of the country village and its inhabitants lay depths of primitive savagery which disrupt their hoped-for idyllic life with violent and startling suddenness. It is an exciting and action-packed story of stunning suspense and involvement. (SPC Doyle, 1971)

Straw Dogs poster, 1971

Press reactions testify to the impact the film had, with some following the British line of horror and distaste, others insisting on its artistic success, while many more seemed dazed and confused: 'It is tremendous movie-making', wrote Arthur Knight in the *Saturday Review*. 'It is also tremendously sick-making'; David Denby in the *Atlantic* found it 'hateful but very exciting ... as brilliant as *The Wild Bunch* but harder to defend' (both cited in Fine, 2005, p. 209). The *Greensboro Daily News* proclaimed it the 'finest movie' of the year, 'beautiful, terrifying and absolutely brilliant' (SPC Yardley, 1971). The same critic chose to interpret it as a celebration of one man's rite of passage from impotent pacifism to justified rage and violent retaliation: 'Violence is, to Peckinpah, a necessary and natural ritual of men in groups. ... a part of the passage to self-fulfillment [sic] and manhood' he wrote, relating it back to *The Wild Bunch* in this respect (SPC Yardley, 1971). The *Newsweek* review trotted out a similar line, declaring that the movie 'flawlessly expresses [Peckinpah's] primitive vision of experience – his belief that manhood requires rites of violence ... that a man must conquer other men to prove his courage and hold on to his woman' (SPC Zimmerman, 1971, p. 87). Winfred Blevins followed suit, headlining her review, '"Straw Dogs": Peckinpah's Assault on Pacifism' (SPC Blevins, 1971).

The reviews seem to have stung Peckinpah, who drafted a number of letters in response. Replying to a review in the *Observer* in the UK (28 November 1971), Peckinpah wrote at some length to the author, film critic George Melly: 'STRAW DOGS concerns a seemingly peaceful man's discovery of the violence within himself, and indirectly his inate [sic] penchant for inciting violence and I hope that this discovery is shared by the audience ...' (SPC Peckinpah, 1971g). Peckinpah evidently saw Sumner as a far more deeply compromised character than many of his reviewers had understood him to be. A draft letter to Dick Schickel is more explicit in this regard: 'I was astonished in your review that you didn't pick up that Dustin was the heavy,' Peckinpah wrote (SPC Peckinpah, 1971i).

However, a number of key critics *did* seem to be in tune with the ambivalence to violence that Peckinpah claimed was his own preoccupation: Kathleen Carroll, though sceptical about the plausibility of aspects of character and plot, conceded that nevertheless 'we are gripped by the film's horrifying climax ... Peckinpah forces us to confront our very own attitudes toward violence' (SPC Carroll, 1972); Jay Cocks (*Time* magazine) suggested that the film challenged 'the very ideal of heroism around which his [Peckinpah's] work so far has been built' (SPC Cocks, 1971, p. 85). While a number of critics in the UK would attack the film for supposed gratuitousness, Bruce Cook was unequivocal in his review for the *National Observer*, running it with the headline, 'The Sex and Violence Are Justified in Peckinpah's Tense "Straw Dogs"', and admitting that 'Anything less than the bloodbath of the last reel would have left me dissatisfied' (SPC Cook, 1972). Although Vincent Canby found the shooting and editing of the siege confusing, he also agreed that the sequence 'serve[d] a dramatic function in a film that seriously attempts to define the meaning of manhood in such terms' (SPC Canby, 1972a).

Undoubtedly the film's most notorious contemporaneous review was written by Pauline Kael. Her labelling of *Straw Dogs* as 'the first American film that is a fascist work of art' (Kael, 1972, p. 84) left the movie with a stigma it has never been able to shake. Peckinpah was incensed: 'How you can identify any element of my work in terms of fascism is beyond my belief and a red flag', he snapped back. He took her to task for failing to decode the film's more subtle subtext: 'I was distressed that you didn't pick up that David was enciting [sic] the very violence he was running away from', he wrote (SPC Peckinpah, 1971h). Kael would later play down the significance of the 'fascist' epithet and insist that it applied strictly to the film's representation of sexuality, which she disliked intensely (Fine, 2005, p. 211). It is notable that very few of the (mostly male) US critics found the rape scene problematic when reviewing the film on its opening. Of course, the figure of Amy would come to dominate discussion of the film in the years ahead, but it seemed to be the siege, rather than the rape scene, that proved the key talking point in the early reviews. Some of the reviews – even some of the fullest and most perceptive ones, such as William Johnson's (1972) in *Film Quarterly* – barely mention the rape. Those that did, did not necessarily take it very seriously. The *National Observer* described 'the notorious "rape"' as only half that' (SPC Cook, 1972); the *New York Times* saw it as 'the toughest – and most erotic scene in the film' (SPC Canby, 1972a); and the *San Francisco Chronicle* characterised it as 'more a rough seduction than a rape' (SPC Knickerbocker, 1971). Jay Cocks was of a similar mind, describing Susan George as 'all teasing, feline sexuality', implying an 'asking-for-it' interpretation (SPC Cocks, 1971, p. 87).

Such comments are indicative of how slowly attitudes were changing towards women and female sexuality, even in the midst of a rising tide of feminist critique of contemporary culture. These attitudes are both symptomatic of and contributory factors to the controversy that would arise around the behaviour and treatment of Amy, and will be explored further in Part 3 (see pp. 86–98).

Sixties Britain: A Quieter Revolution

As we have seen, the few years preceding the release of *Straw Dogs* constituted a time of massive social upheaval in the United States. While America rocked in the 60s, England was swinging somewhat more gently: demonstrations did take place, notably anti-Vietnam rallies of some 10,000 in London in October 1967 and 20,000 in March 1968, but, for the most part, London was, in Peter Doggett's words, 'the vacuum of late 1960s rebellion' (Doggett, 2007, p. 167). On the other hand, the British political and legal system did reflect some profound, if more gradual, cultural shifts, particularly, as in America, in terms of attitudes towards the place of women and understandings of sexual identity and sexual practices. The year 1967 saw the passing of the Abortion Act, the National Health Service (Family Planning) Act and the Sexual Offences Act (beginning the process of legalising homosexuality); the Divorce Reform Act followed in 1969 and the Matrimonial Property Act in 1970 (Aldgate and Robertson, 2005, p. 129). However, just as in the US, as the decade turned, there were clear signs of a political sea-change brewing: the election of Richard Nixon as President in 1968 was mirrored by the return to power of the Conservative Party under Edward Heath in the general election of June 1970.

A swing back towards cultural conservatism could be observed not just in the mechanics of party-political change, however. An organisation that took the name the Festival of Light began to hit the headlines as the new decade dawned, an alliance that included such high-profile figures as Lord Longford, Christian writer and broadcaster Malcolm Muggeridge and campaigner Mary Whitehouse, who in 1965 had established the National Viewers' and Listeners' Association pressure group. An explicitly Christian organisation, whose activities included a march on Trafalgar Square on 25 September 1971 attracting tens of thousands of people, the Festival of Light represented the most visible marker of what has been described as a silent majority (but might, as others have noted, be more accurately described as a vocal minority). Other groups working with a similar agenda included the Responsible Society, led by family doctor S. E. Ellison (Sandbrook, 2006, p. 551) and Lord Longford's Commission on Pornography (1971–2), which made forceful claims about the dangers to individuals and to society as a whole of sexually explicit material. The targets of these clean-up organisations, then, were supposed declines in moral standards and the spread of permissiveness in society, particularly amongst the young. The voice of the political-social-cultural right was often louder, and certainly more coherent, than the left, and it found willing allies in certain sectors of the British press, both in the populist tabloids and the broadsheets. In this climate, the British Board of Film Censors was a convenient target, and John Trevelyan, Secretary of the BBFC from 1958 until 1971, found himself waging a complex, exhausting campaign on two fronts in his latter years in the post.

By 1971, the thorny problem of sex on film was becoming more troublesome, in terms of both volume (with an exponential increase in the number of films submitted to the BBFC containing representations of sexual activity) and in terms of explicitness. Trevelyan took up his post just after the Obscene Publications Act was passed in Parliament (covering England and Wales, but not Scotland and the North of Ireland), a law that signalled a cultural shift usually marked in histories of censorship by the *Lady Chatterley's Lover* court case of 1960, when the publishers of D. H. Lawrence's sexually explicit novel were acquitted of obscenity charges. The successful defence of the novel was grounded in the Act's 'public good' exemption, which made allowances if the publication of the work in question was deemed to be 'in the interests of science, literature, art or learning, or of other objects of general concern'.

Trevelyan found himself negotiating often very delicate dilemmas at a time when an imprecise system was forced to cope with an overwhelming flood of material that would have been unimaginable ten (or even five) years earlier. Trevelyan's predecessor, John Nichols, had maintained an already familiar practice of policing foreign-language films much less harshly, an attitude that has arguably remained a more or less overt BBFC policy ever since it published a pamphlet deliberating over the dangers of presenting troubling images to 'the average audience which includes a not inconsiderable proportion of people of immature judgement' (cited in Davy, 1938, p. 141). The first full-frontal female nudity had graced UK screens in 1968, via the Swedish director Jonas Cornell's *Hugs and Kisses* – originally cut at Trevelyan's request, but restored after he had waved similar shots through in Lindsay

Anderson's politically subversive movie *If….* (1968). Trevelyan had also shown himself keen to do what he could to support the work of avant-garde film-makers such as Andy Warhol and his associates: Warhol's movie *Flesh* (1968), which follows a day in the life of a male prostitute in New York City, had been refused a certificate, but, in a gesture intended to support both film-makers and theatre practitioners, Trevelyan recommended that the distributor, Jimmy Vaughan, screen it in a private club setting in London, linking Vaughan up with the Open Space Theatre run by Thelma Holt and the American playwright and director Charles Marowitz. The project backfired in February 1970 when police raided the club during a screening of *Flesh*. Trevelyan reacted angrily to the intervention, arguing that the 'Open Space Theatre was a reputable theatre club, supported by the Arts Council, with a membership of intellectuals'; he went on to argue that, in his view, 'the film was entirely suitable for showing to audiences of this kind but would have little interest or profitability in commercial cinemas' (Trevelyan, 1973, p. 130), echoing the ideological slant of the BBFC pamphlet quoted above. In the end, there was no case to be answered, since the Obscene Publications Act at that time did not apply to the medium of film. The theatre was, rather spitefully, fined £200 for admitting non members to the screening, a sum that Warhol eventually paid himself. Later that year, Vaughan wrote Trevelyan a letter robustly supporting his decision to award *Straw Dogs* a certificate, amidst the storm of press controversy and letters from the public.

Liberalising efforts are also discernible in the changes applied to the BBFC's certification process in 1970: the introduction of an 'AA' certificate (14+ years) in July of that year was significant, but there had also been a more gradual shift in the conception of the 'X' certificate, which had, until 1970, specified suitability for audiences of 16+ years only. During the latter years of the preceding decade, it had come to be associated with bolder, often experimental, foreign-language films and – by implication if not always in fact – with sex. However, a rising tide of films in the social-realism tradition had, some time earlier, marked an impetus to treat sexuality with a new degree of frankness – if not in terms of graphic imagery, at least in terms of language:

Look Back in Anger (1958), *Room at the Top* (1959) and *A Taste of Honey* (1961) had kickstarted the trend, and more were to follow over the next few years, notably *Up the Junction* (1967) and *The Killing of Sister George* (1968), which was ground-breaking in its portrayal of lesbian relationships. This trend had led inevitably to a more frequent use of the 'X' certificate by the BBFC. Paradoxically, however, the shift from 16+ to 18+ for the classification in 1970 had not been an attempt to be more restrictive, but rather signalled the Board's intention to loosen restrictions, since it had made the decision under the presumption that it would mean very few films submitted to the BBFC would require any censorship at all – a naive hope, as it would turn out. John Trevelyan admits in his memoir that:

> We were optimistic in thinking that the raising of the minimum age for 'X' films from sixteen to eighteen would make censorship of films for this category virtually unnecessary. By the time the new system was introduced many films contained material that could not be passed even for adult audiences, reflecting the abolition or weakening of controls in various other countries. If the age had not been raised a far larger number of films would have had to be refused certificates, but even so the Board still found it necessary to ban certain films entirely and to continue to make cuts in 'X' films. (Trevelyan, 1973, p. 64)

Alexander Walker notes that this sense of a mounting crisis was made more acute when Trevelyan returned from a convention of US cinema owners with the announcement that, 'The porn market in America has almost completely replaced the nude market' (Walker, 1985, p. 32). By December 1970, Trevelyan had announced his retirement from his post, confessing in an interview with the *Evening Standard* that he was 'sickened by having to put in days filled from dawn to dusk with the sight and sound of human copulation' (cited in Walker, 1985, p. 33). At the same time, just as in New York City, private cinemas showing unlicensed pornographic movies were on the increase in the capital.

The BBFC file on *Straw Dogs* includes a long-running series of letters between new BBFC Secretary Stephen Murphy and a correspondent I will refer to as RCB of Sevenoaks, Kent, who had written protesting the Board's decision to grant it a certificate. One of Murphy's replies pointed out the two horns of the dilemma upon which he found himself perched:

> You really must accept that the British Board of Film Censors is under fire in two directions. On the one hand there is a very strongly expressed view that all film censorship should be abolished, just as the Lord Chamberlain's power of censorship over the theatre was abolished. This would admit to this country a flood of films the like of which you have not seen nor heard of. On the other hand there is a group like yourself calling for stricter censorship and we poor middle of the roaders who try to exercise some kind of intelligent judgement are in danger of being knocked down by the haste with which the traffic goes by on either side of us. (bbfc Murphy, 1972)

In 1971, that traffic included three particularly heavy juggernauts. Hard on the heels of *Straw Dogs* would come *A Clockwork Orange* (1971), but, preceding both of them, Ken Russell's *The Devils* (1971) had already provided an excuse for the Festival of Light and associated groups to turn their attention to the business of the BBFC. Russell's film was an adaptation of Aldous Huxley's *The Devils of Loudon* (1952), the tale of a seventeenth-century French priest burned at the stake for the crime of seducing a convent of nuns in his parish. The movie was released in the UK in July 1971, but had already caused controversy with lurid tales from the set (it had been filmed at Pinewood and a number of other English locations). The combined potential for blasphemy and explicit sexual content made the film a convenient target for these conservative morality pressure groups, and they lobbied the BBFC hard to have the 'X' certificate withdrawn and *The Devils* banned from distribution. Russell's counter-attack was shrewdly strategised around a claim that he had made what he protested was 'a deeply religious film' (cited in

Phelps, 1975, p. 75). When Stephen Murphy stood firm against the pressure groups, they adopted a new approach, targeting the Greater London Council. Although the GLC was persuaded to arrange a private viewing of the film, its decision was to endorse the BBFC ruling. According to the chairman of the GLC's film-viewing subcommittee, 'It was not within [its] purview ... to ban the film, the policy being to accept films passed by the B.B.F.C.' (cited in Phelps, 1975, p. 76). However, the gap between the BBFC and local councils in terms of potential bans had started to open up, and the film was subsequently banned by a number of other local councils. At the time of writing, it remains unavailable on home-video format in the UK.

Straw Dogs presented Stephen Murphy with a particular problem in terms of the representation of sexual activity. The story is a salutary reminder of the perils of censorship. Having seen the first cut of the movie in August 1971, and having discussed it in detail with Dan Melnick, Murphy made a number of requests for cuts, including some significant editing of the second rape. Once the cuts had been made, the film was returned for a second viewing. A note from the examiners reported that 'The rape scene was our chief anxiety' and that 'The Secretary decided to discuss possible reduction, as well as interpretation of the second part of the action, with the Company' (bbfc Anon, 1971). The inadvertent outcome of the edits had been to cause some confusion over the kind of sexual abuse Scutt perpetrates. Bluntly put, the question is whether the act is rear-entry or anal rape. The note in the BBFC archive is annotated at a later, undetermined date, and explains that, 'This impression [anal rape] is a result of the Company's cuts to reduce the sequence to help us' (bbfc Anon, 1971) (the note appears to be initialled by Stephen Murphy). It would seem that a member of Peckinpah's editing team was called in to discuss the matter, as on 10 November, Murphy wrote to Melnick: 'my Examiners have much dirtier minds than I have; however, your Editor was able to resolve our doubts as to the exact direction of assault on Miss George, and there are no problems left'. He also remarks that, 'I have seen the whole film twice, parts of it three times, and it still makes me tremble about the knees' (bbfc Murphy, 1971a). Reflecting on the confusion

arising from the unfortunate edit, Murphy remarked ruefully in his
annotation to the original censors' notes that 'Alas, we've already cut the
optical track so I fear there is nothing we can do about it, save a show of
righteous indignation when accused' (bbfc Anon, 1971). A letter in response
to RCB is more detailed:

> I must take some responsibility for the act of 'buggery' (it isn't, even
> technically!). I told the producer that in my view the rape scene was, as I
> originally saw it, far too long – giving, it seemed to me, the feeling that
> the film was wallowing in it. The whole sequence was re-edited and I
> must confess that until it was pointed out to me I hadn't spotted that the
> drastic shortening had led to this impression – a false one, I do assure
> you. (bbfc Murphy, 1971b)

What had been intended when the scene was shot in fact remains moot,
although it would seem that Melnick had made the very sensible decision to
maintain that it was *not* anal rape, realising that such a thing would have been
beyond the pale for the staff of the BBFC offices (Melnick contacted Stephen
Murphy subsequently, noting courteously – or perhaps with tongue in cheek –
'You have an enormously difficult job, and you discharge your professional
obligations in such a reasonable and constructive manner that it is almost a
pleasure to be "censored"' [bbfc Melnick, 1971]). Whatever might have been
intended, the attempt to censor such sensitive sexual material had done
nothing but create a more complex controversy.

Straw Dogs and the UK Critics

Straw Dogs opened in the UK on 25 November 1971, and it was greeted with
a barrage of hostility, spearheaded by the majority of the respected London
press film critics, notably Alexander Walker (for the *Evening Standard*) and
Margaret Hinxman for the *Sunday Telegraph*. The latter chose to contrast it

unfavourably with *The Wild Bunch*. According to Hinxman, the context for the violence in *Straw Dogs* was so implausible that it rendered any attempt to preach a message about violence meaningless, with the result that the film was nothing more than 'sadistic porn ... a badly made film with nothing to say' (bbfc Hinxman, 1971). David Robinson, reviewing for the *Financial Times*, suggested that, 'the violence is presented as entirely laudable and justified in its own terms', arguing that the film's 'unequivocal message' is that Sumner's violent response is the only way he can 'regain his self-respect and the respect of his wife' (bbfc Robinson, 1971). Alexander Walker, in what was probably the most venomous of the reviews, declared that 'Not one point which [the film] might have made about violence breeding counter-violence ... is credibly or adequately made by this raw presentation of salacity and mayhem' (bbfc Walker, 1971). Using his indignation as a springboard to launch an assault on the BBFC, he added,

> What the film censor has permitted on screen in *Straw Dogs* makes one wonder whether he has any further useful role to play in the cinema industry ... . To pass it on for public exhibition in its present form is tantamount to a dereliction of duty. For if this goes, then anything goes.

John Coleman (1971) described it as 'two hours of gratuitous violence, sexual and otherwise' and declared that Stephen Murphy had 'certified himself out of a function' by passing it for exhibition; Tony Palmer (*Spectator*) dismissed it as 'a tale of bestiality, murder, rape, arson, buggery, lechery, incest and idiocy' (cited in Barr, 1972, p. 19).[23] The *Financial Times* critic believed that 'the violence is presented as entirely laudable and justifiable in its own terms' (bbfc Robinson, 1971). Negative reviews were also published in the *Daily Telegraph* (bbfc Gibbs, 1971), *News of the World* and *Observer* (George Melly). Dilys Powell concluded her damning review with the words, 'For the first time in my life I felt concern for the future of the cinema' (bbfc Powell, 1971).

On 17 December, a letter appeared in the London *Times* signed by thirteen critics, condemning the film by arguing that the use to which it

> employs its scenes of double rape and multiple killings by a variety of hideous methods is dubious in its intention, excessive in its effect and likely to contribute to the concern expressed from time to time by many critics over films which exploit the very violence which they make a show of condemning.[24] (cited in Phelps, 1975, p. 78)

The letter went on to invite the BBFC to justify how it could reconcile its attitude towards the Warhol film *Trash* (1970) (denied a certificate because of a reluctance to suggest that drugs could be seen as a 'natural or acceptable part of the contemporary scene') with its response to *Straw Dogs:* 'Is violence a more acceptable part of the scene, in the censor's eyes, than drugs?', they demanded (cited in Phelps, 1975, p. 79). At the populist end of the press, Fergus Cashin wrote an article for the *Sun* entitled 'Why Can't I Take My Family to the Pictures?', which took Murphy to task for what he saw as an attack on public standards of decency: 'He [Murphy] and he alone opened the floodgates of pornographic violence as depicted in the gang rapes of *Clockwork Orange*, and the obscure sadism of *Straw Dogs*', Cashin wrote. 'If Stephen Murphy must continue as censor, let him be strong enough to go on the studio floor and warn the film-makers, face to face, that the public will not tolerate mindless pornographic violence' (bbfc Cashin, 1972). Murphy and the BBFC President Lord Harlech's considered response to the *Times* letter offers a robust riposte to all of this, describing a screening of the film before an invited audience chosen to represent all sectors of the population, and noting that a majority of them 'disagreed with the [*Times* letter's] critics strictures of the film' and that 'the board's decision to certificate it was not seriously questioned' (bbfc Murphy and Harlech, 1971). They also noted the certification status in the US, where it could be seen by children accompanied by adults (but failed to mention that the MPAA had insisted on significant cuts before granting it an 'R' rating).

Some writers have suggested that the film drew such rancour from British newspaper critics previously supportive of Peckinpah not only for its depiction of violence, but also for its less than complimentary representation of rural England: many reviewers were disparaging with regard to the film's 'realism'; Gavin Millar's sniffy remark that 'Peckinpah's acquaintance with English life, let alone rural and regional life, is unsurpassedly faint' was typical (cited in Barr, 1972, p. 20). Margaret Hinxman was under the impression that Peckinpah had exported his Western milieu to the West Country, and was of the opinion that 'the natives in that loveliest and most reserved of English counties have far more subtle means of freezing a stranger' than besieging his home (bbfc Hinxman, 1971). Dilys Powell interpreted it as a translation of 'the Sioux or the Apache massacre from the Western to an English living-room', but added that 'no redskin attack, no paleface revenge I ever saw on the screen was as mindlessly revolting' (bbfc Powell, 1971). David Robinson described the inhabitants of Wakely as 'a violent and unlovely lot of idiots, rapists, nymphomaniacs and drunks' (bbfc Robinson, 1971). It's worth noting that many early drafts of the script referred to underage sex and depicted a much less ambiguous incestuous relationship between Janice and Bobby Hedden; the 'as-shot' shooting script even includes dialogue between Major Scott and David as they drive out to the farmhouse in which Scott discusses the inbreeding in Wakely (SPC G&P 1971c, pp. 53–4).[25] Another draft includes a reference to Henry Niles 'hav[ing] his way' with Janice after he has accidentally killed her – which presumably either Goodman, Peckinpah or both considered a step too far. One can only imagine the press reaction had necrophilia been added to the movie's catalogue of horrors.

Murphy, under fire from the press and facing a stream of letters from concerned members of the public, stood by the film, insistent that it was a serious attempt to say something meaningful about violence. He argued the point with a number of individuals who had written to the BBFC, including RCB, mentioned above. Murphy was adamant that

> We at the Board will do all we can to stop film-makers exploiting violence:
> but when a serious film-maker makes a serious film about violence, I think
> we would be failing in our public duty if we prevented people from seeing
> it – however unpopular our decision may be. (bbfc Murphy 1971b)

RCB's concerns about 'young folk likely to be harmed by the film's atrocious portrayal of sexual sadism – double rape – & other monstrous indecencies' (bbfc RCB, 1972; emphasis in the original) were dismissed by Murphy, who argued that the film was more likely to act as a deterrent than an incentive to violence.

However, *Straw Dogs,* together with *The Devils* and *A Clockwork Orange* – another film featuring shocking sexualised violence – had stirred controversies that would reverberate throughout the decade, as moral conservatism battled against a progressive agenda. Several local city, town and county councils refused to grant permission for the screening of *Straw Dogs* in cinemas licensed under their jurisdiction until they had viewed it themselves. Outcomes varied: in Surrey, the film was only permitted to be shown with the entire rape scene excised; Newcastle upon Tyne granted a licence; Manchester and Salford and RCB's hometown of Sevenoaks, Kent refused permission for any public performances of the film (the latter ban was not lifted until 1974). Within a year, *Trash* would be granted a certificate and *Last Tango in Paris* (1972) would raise further questions about graphic representations of sexual activity – the controversy over the anal sex scene traceable back to the trouble caused for censors and editors by the second rape in *Straw Dogs.* In the wake of increasing liberalism by the BBFC, a backlash developed from the grassroots, and councils across the nation would challenge the BBFC's hegemony by banning a number of films granted certificates by the Board. Largely, it seems, this was due to what Julian Petley likens to 'a game of Chinese whispers' (Petley, 2002, p. 39), where local councillors, in all likelihood, 'felt able to deliver their verdicts on the film without the benefit of having seen it' (Phelps, 1975, cited in Petley, 2002, p. 39). Ironically, even the BBFC found itself faltering in response to a rising tide of imported films characterised by excessive acts of violence, often sexualised: Phelps notes that the Board 'responded by indulging in some of the most brutal cuttings and banning in its history' (1975, p. 126). Its panicky reaction eerily anticipates the trouble it would face over ten years later with the rise of the so-called 'video nasties'. With *Straw Dogs* a notable casualty of that controversy, too, there is a provocative, if depressing circularity to the debate, which is explored further in the section that follows.

✕ Part 2

STRAW DOGS SINCE THEN

Home-Video Release: The Video-Nasties Debate

A full understanding of the reception of popular texts such as films at different cultural moments needs to take account of a variety of sociopolitical factors. However, there are times when other, more unexpected elements can have a considerable impact, such as sudden, traumatic national events: both the immediate and the longer-term consequences of the attack on the World Trade Center on 11 September 2001 for the Hollywood industry, for instance, are well documented; on a smaller scale, as one example from a multitude of possibilities, the home-video release of Oliver Stone's *Natural Born Killers* (1994) was delayed by the distributors in the wake of the murder of schoolchildren in Dunblane, Scotland, on 13 March 1996 and the subsequent revival of concerns over the possible effects of media violence.

Technological change is a constant in the film industry, from the seismic shifts triggered by the move from silent film to 'talkies', to the more subtle changes in special effects: take as an example *The Matrix* (1999), with its 'bullet-time' innovations and its appropriation of wire-work stunts from Asian martial arts movies that reinvigorated Hollywood action cinema at the turn of the millennium. However, sometimes changes in technology in terms of consumption, rather than production of film texts can be equally significant, and one of the most important shifts of the second half of the twentieth century was the rise of the home-video format. The impact of this innovation in the early 1980s was massive at all levels of the industry, but one area of film consumption where its significance could not have been predicted – at least on the scale involved – was the category of films that would come to be known in the UK as 'video nasties'.

The full scale and complex history of the 'video-nasty' debate that erupted in 1983 and 1984 in the UK cannot be documented here.[26] It is enough to note that the increased accessibility to film in the home with the advent of rental and then sell-through video cassettes led to a rising tide of apparent concern about the availability of material unsuitable for children, particularly in terms of representations of violence. The problem was compounded by the fact that no certification process was in place to monitor the marketing and distribution of home-video titles. The right-wing press, chiefly though not exclusively via the mid-market tabloids, fanned the flames with its campaign to 'Ban the Sadist Videos' (*Daily Mail*). Even the *Sunday Times* featured stories of 'HOW HIGH STREET HORROR IS INVADING THE HOME' (23 May 1982), and the then secretary of the BBFC, James Ferman, concurred: '[children] are watching shocking scenes that we would never allow in a cinema, even under an "X"-certificate' (both cited in Martin, 2007, p. 14). What followed was a peculiarly British conflation of press hysteria, political opportunism and institutional intervention, as a government eager to prove its law, order and decency credentials seized upon the issue and began to turn it into a staging post on the route towards the moral high ground. A working party was set up between the British Videogram Association (the video distributors' organisation) and the BBFC, with a view to establishing a system of classifying home video. In the meantime, there were attempts to establish a precedent to prosecute material already in circulation under the Obscene Publications Acts of 1959 and 1964 (which had been expanded to include film in 1977). The films in question covered a range of genres, periods and nationalities, including everything from art-house pieces like *Possession* (1981) to exploitation fare such as *Mardi Gras Massacre* (1978) and *S.S. Experiment Camp* (1976). With pressure building on the Director of Public Prosecutions to take a hard line on the distributors of the videos, by August 1982, the DPP was extending an offer to the companies: destroy their master tapes and cease distribution and so avoid prosecution. While many complied with the request, others continued to distribute and supply titles that had been included on the DPP's initial 'hit list' of fifty-two films, with the first successful prosecution of a distribution company in February 1984. Having previously resolved to allow the industry to regulate itself, the Tory government identified the 'video-nasty' debate as a potential vote-winner, and went into its re-election campaign trumpeting its intention to introduce tighter control via parliamentary legislation.

Eighteen Years in the Wilderness

How did a movie like *Straw Dogs* – made on a Hollywood budget, with a global, Academy-Award-nominated star and respected director, become tangled up in a loose conglomeration of films that, for the most part, had little in common with each other beside their graphic violence, poor acting, directing and writing, and low production values? Although Peckinpah's film was never included on the DPP's hit list, the reasons why it was effectively banned in the UK for about twenty years are bound up in the press panics, changes in legislation and the evolving role of the BBFC in the certification of home video that were brought about by the 'video-nasty' scare of the 1980s. *Straw Dogs* also had the misfortune of becoming something of an obsession for BBFC Secretary (later Director) James Ferman, who succeeded Stephen Murphy in 1975. Ferman was essentially a liberal, but, while, on the one hand, his tenure would see a considerable relaxation of attitudes towards representations of sexuality, on the other, his abhorrence of sexual violence (and his apparent tendency to favour the appointment of examiners who shared his perspective) was a defining factor in many censorship and certification decisions in the 70s, 80s and 90s. Largely because of Ferman's attitude towards Peckinpah's film, *Straw Dogs* would become a fixture in the BBFC offices for many years, required viewing for newly appointed examiners as a test case exploring the boundaries of what was and was not deemed acceptable at the time.

    Guild Home Video first released a VHS rental version of *Straw Dogs* in 1980.[27] Although, as I have indicated, no formal process for video certification was in place at this point, the cover art included an indicator of its original 'X'-certificate rating; the same packaging also, somewhat confusingly,

Having refused to countenance a video release in the late 1980s, on 20 April 1995, the BBFC passed a version submitted by the British Film Institute for *cinema* exhibition, granting it an '18' certificate. However, the BFI had submitted the pre-cut, US version in error, meaning that the film in its uncut form was still unavailable in the UK (this version had a runtime of 116 minutes 2 seconds and a length of 10,443 feet and 11 frames).[28] When in September of the same year, Polygram asked the BBFC to reconsider certifying a version of *Straw Dogs* for home-video release, Ferman refused, citing the changes to the regulations made in 1994 when the Home Video Recordings Act was modified by the Criminal Justice and Public Order Act. The Act required the BBFC to pay particular attention to the content of films that might 'have the potential to cause harm to viewers or, through their behaviour, to society' by the way they represent a range of things, including 'violent behaviour or incidents' and 'human sexual activity'. According to the BBFC guidelines, the Video Recordings Act also required the Board to 'have special regard to' home viewing: the fact that home video allowed viewers to replay particular scenes out of context over and over again was perceived as a major problem (another new challenge presented by technological changes). According to the BBFC's own summary of the *Straw Dogs* case, this was 'particularly problematic' in relation to Peckinpah's film, 'because Amy's ambiguous reaction to the rape could be viewed out of the wider context of the film, fuelling the fantasies of potential offenders' (BBFC, undated). For nearly ten years, *Straw Dogs* would remain without an official release in the UK, circulating in bootleg form amongst collectors.

The next rights holder, Total Home Ent (London) submitted the American 'R'-rated version, which cut almost all of the second rape, in 1996, pressing Ferman for a verdict despite his advice to withdraw the submission. Between 1997 and 1998, the 'R'-rated cut was reportedly viewed by every BBFC examiner, and viewed again by the incoming BBFC President, Andreas Whittam Smith. It appears that the response from examiners now was that this version, which removed most of the sequence in which Scutt rapes Amy, was in some ways more problematic, since it tended to endorse the 'rape myth',

discussed elsewhere, giving the impression that in certain circumstances
women may enjoy being raped.[29] Letters from two psychologists, reporting to
Ferman on their impressions of the uncut version, offer divergent conclusions.
One, while confessing he would 'happily throw [the film] in the bin', conceded
that he did not believe there to be 'any psychiatric or psychological ground' for
not licensing the film uncut. However, the other expressed 'concern' over the
first rape, which he described as 'a classic rape myth promoter ... I would be a
lot happier', he concluded, 'if the scene was further cut so that it gave the
impression that the woman was disgusted with the activities that were
happening to her' in both rape scenes.[30]

Things became even more complex when, with Ferman about to retire
and deferring a decision again, Video Collection International submitted the
uncut version of the film, as originally seen in UK cinemas for consideration.
In January 1999, Robin Duval succeeded James Ferman as Secretary of the
BBFC, and in March he offered an '18' home-video certificate to the 'R'-rated
version on the condition that approximately three minutes of the rape scene
were cut ('principally to remove the forcible nudity and the indications of
pleasure at being raped', according to the press release [Whittam Smith and
Duval, 1999]). By this time, however, Total Home Ent's rights had expired,
and once again no further progress was made. On 15 March 1999, THE's 'R'-
rated version was formally rejected, and on 2 June the VCI (uncut) version
suffered the same fate.

The press release announcing the decision spelled out the principle that
'Sexual violence may only be shown providing the scenes do not offer sexual
thrills.' It itemised the precise difficulties in detail:

> The first is the fact that the rapes are clearly effected by violence and the
> threat of violence. The second is the extent of the erotic content, notably
> Amy's forcible stripping and nudity. The third element of concern is the
> clear indication that Amy comes to enjoy being raped. It is Board policy
> not to condone material which endorses the well-known male rape myth
> that 'women like it really'.

The Board concluded that 'the video was potentially harmful because of the influence it may have on the attitudes and behaviour of a significant proportion of its likely viewers' (Whittam Smith and Duval, 1999). In its annual report, the statement was even more direct, expressing the concern bluntly that 'the sequence was filmed in a manner which could arouse some viewers' (BBFC, 1999, p. 21). In September 1999, Whittam Smith, in an interview for the *Guardian* newspaper, seemed to draw a thick line under the topic, stating that he believed that the rape scene in *Straw Dogs* 'fits precisely into the Video Recording Act's definition of harm'. He argued that, 'It shows that a woman who first resists will then comply and that "no" really means "yes" and therefore conveys the clear message that violence for the male will bring its reward. That's very clear,' he concluded, 'and that's why I think we could not ever pass it' (Whittam Smith, 1999).

Moving with the Times: The BBFC and Sexual Violence

In the wake of these apparently definitive statements, it seems paradoxical that the turn of the century witnessed something of a revolution in terms of the BBFC's attitude towards its role, and its relation with the cinemagoing, and video-watching public. In the face of criticisms that it was increasingly out of touch with changes in public attitudes, the Board attempted a rapprochement with filmgoers via consultation exercises, and these resulted in new guidelines for video certification being drawn up. The findings of one such exercise, *Sense and Sensibilities: Public Opinion and the BBFC Guidelines*, were published in September 2000 (bbfc Hanley, 2000). More pertinently – and probably largely in an attempt to deal with the recurrent issue of *Straw Dogs* – the BBFC commissioned a study of attitudes towards sexual violence. Published in 2002 under the title *Where Do You Draw the Line?*, the report claimed to be an in-depth survey of '*Attitudes and Reactions of Video Renters to Sexual Violence in Film*'. A team led by Dr Guy Cumberbatch investigated a group selected from video renters in the Midlands area of the UK.

Cumberbatch had been one of the authors of the 1990 Home Office Research Unit's report on *Pornography: Impacts and Influences*, which had been commissioned by Margaret Thatcher's government, and promptly shelved upon submission because the findings were far more liberal than Home Secretary Kenneth Baker would have liked.[31] Cumberbatch's new project, exploring attitudes towards representations of sexual violence, began with a short questionnaire, from which 277 forms were sampled, and as the research proceeded a focus group of twenty-six people viewed a number of films featuring graphic representations of sexual violence: *A Clockwork Orange*, *Straw Dogs*, *The Last House on the Left*, *Death Wish II*, *I Spit on Your Grave* and *Baise-Moi* (2000).

Although flawed,[32] the findings were still fascinating for a number of reasons, not the least of which was that, in the first place, a striking proportion of respondents believed that adults did not necessarily have the right to see sexual violence in films and videos: 'While the great majority believed that adults have a right to see graphic violence (74%) and graphic sex (67%), it dropped to a minority of only 38% for sexual violence', the report noted (Cumberbatch, 2002, p. 7). In the second place, actually viewing sexual violence seemed to result in less rather than more liberal expressions of opinion about what was acceptable. In other words, viewing such material had an aversive effect rather than the opposite, apparently contradicting the 'common sense' of the pro-censorship lobby, with its concerns about imitative violence and desensitisation. What was perhaps most interesting with regard to *Straw Dogs* was the way in which it seemed simply to fade into the background over the course of the discussions that followed. Its violence was nowhere near commensurate with some of the more brutal scenes in the films it was viewed alongside, such as *I Spit on Your Grave* and *Baise-Moi*. When asked whether they believed *Straw Dogs* was suitable for release on video, 77 per cent said they believed it was acceptable, 19 per cent suggested minor cuts and 4 per cent (i.e. one viewer from a group of twenty-six) felt it was unsuitable for release. No-one believed that major cuts should be made along the lines required by the Board when considering the 1999 video-certification submission.

Both the Cumberbatch research and the more recent study led by Martin Barker suggest that 'the acceptability and availability of an individual scene of strong sexual violence is not accepted as the norm but is heavily dependant [sic] on the nature, tone, narrative and other contexts of the work' (BBFC, 2007, p. 74). In addition, Martin Barker's project investigating audience response to the film reinforces the fact that even methodical, qualitative analysis tends not to yield easily analysable, 'enactable' results. Barker rightly critiqued the Cumberbatch report for its vagueness over some crucial parameters and its tendency towards setting 'leading' questions for the respondents. Barker was much less dogmatic, allowing a greater 'openness' in the questions asked, and allowing those taking part to offer their own definitions of their viewing experiences. His clear conclusion was that

> there is not *a* reading of a film, and that to assume that audiences watch films in order to decipher specific 'messages' is erroneous and does not take into account the high degree of variability in strategies of reading film, and the conclusions reached by different viewers. (Barker, 2005, p. 35)

If Barker's research tells us nothing else definitively – and he is himself clear that what he is doing is not trying to draw conclusions about reception of the film specifically, but merely 'trying to identify the *processes involved in forming a judgement of any kind*' (p. 37) – it does at least warn us that we cannot generalise about what viewers bring to the experience of watching a film any more than we can generalise about responses to it.

It was in the context of Cumberbatch's study, ongoing at the time, as well as in the teeth of the apparently permanent ban on *Straw Dogs* announced in 1999, that Ken Law, Head of Marketing at Fremantle Media, made the decision to resubmit the uncut version for home-video certification in July 2001. Law was not only committed to the release of this particular title (he referred to it as 'a personal crusade' [Anon, imdb, 2002]), but was motivated by a determination to challenge the BBFC's practice of censorship more widely, questioning their reasoning as well as their processes. Correspondence between Peter Woods and senior BBFC examiner Craig Lapper at the BBFC suggests that the Board was at this time still basing its decisions to demand cuts around the issues of 'endorsing' and 'eroticising' sexual assault (Lapper cites *Baise-Moi* as an example of the latter, and *Straw Dogs* as an example of the former) (Lapper, 2001). Ken Law had been discussing the film with Lapper for several months, and he had been advised that, while the Board would be prepared to pass a cut version, an insistence on an uncut submission would most likely end up before the Video Appeals Committee, which would make its own independent judgement. Law was determined to proceed regardless, and Lapper informed Robin Duval of Law's firm intention to submit the film in its uncut form, and to go to appeal if necessary. It is likely that this influenced the Board's decision to take stock and make a concerted effort to deal with *Straw Dogs*, despite the fact that it had been refused uncut certification very recently (a decision endorsed publicly by Whittam Smith in the *Guardian* interview – sec p. 60). Three clinical psychologists with expertise in dealing with sex offenders were shown the uncut film, and they expressed a view that this version 'was not harmful and was not likely to encourage an interest in rape or abusive behaviour towards women' (BBFC, 2002a). The press release announcing an uncut '18' certificate would also note that the previous submission of what it refers to as 'The pre-cut American version' was problematic because it had

> deleted most of the second rape in which Amy is clearly demonstrated not to enjoy the act of violation. The cuts made for American distribution, which were made to reduce the duration of the sequence, therefore tended paradoxically to compound the difficulty with the first rape, leaving the audience with the impression that Amy enjoyed the experience. The Board took the view in 1999 that the pre-cut version eroticised the rape and therefore conflicted with the concerns expressed in the Video Recordings Act about promoting harmful activity. (BBFC, 2002a)

The Board noted that the decision by the distributor to submit the original, UK theatrical version (i.e. 'uncut') 'had the perhaps unexpected effect of moderating earlier concerns', since this version did not leave 'the misleading (and dangerous) impression that the woman involved actually enjoyed being raped' (BBFC, 2002b, p. 13). The press release also emphasised strongly the significance of context, noting that 'the ambiguity of the first rape is given context by the second rape, which now makes it quite clear that sexual assault is not something that Amy ultimately welcomes'. The Board stressed that this was in line with the psychologists' report, who also believed that the scene was filmed 'in a relatively discreet manner, with limited potential today for titillation' (BBFC, 2002a). The respondents in the Cumberbatch study also thought that Amy's flashback experiences after the rape 'reinforced the idea that rape is not to be taken lightly because of the serious effect it can have on individuals' (BBFC, undated). Taking all this into account, the BBFC came to the conclusion that the uncut version of *Straw Dogs* was not in breach of its policy on representations of sexual violence.

In the face of this, then, what was it that brought about a further delay in the classification of *Straw Dogs* for home-video release? The fact that *Last House on the Left* was also under review at the BBFC at the same time probably helped Peckinpah's film in the long run, although it complicated matters in the short term: the very different responses to the two films in the Cumberbatch report meant that the Board could build a strong case against *Last House,* but not necessarily against *Straw Dogs.* When Carl Daft of Blue Underground first submitted *Last House*, he was informed that sixteen seconds of cuts would be required before it could be awarded an '18' certificate. The decision was in line with a BBFC policy dictating that a film that had 'recently' been the subject of a successful prosecution under the Obscene Publications Act (OPA) of 1959 could not be passed uncut (and legal advice had defined 'recently' as within ten years) (slasherama.com [undated]). Rather than making the cuts, Daft chose to appeal the decision, and the Video Appeals Committee hearing to consider the case took place on 23 May 2002. In defence of its demand for cuts, the BBFC quoted not only the Obscene

Publications Act but also the Video Recordings Act (VRA): it claimed that the film contravened the principle of 'potential harm' enshrined in the VRA, and also pointed to other recent research it had commissioned (such as the 2000 *Sense and Sensibilities* survey) that suggested film representations of sexual violence remained a real concern for the British public (see Woods, 2002 for further details of the hearing). The BBFC cited Cumberbatch's research and the specific responses of test audiences to *Last House* (generally far less positive than to *Straw Dogs*): 56 per cent had expressed the opinion that the film should *not* be released uncut, with that figure rising to 85 per cent amongst female respondents.

What makes the connection between *Straw Dogs* and *Last House* even more provocative is the fact that the BBFC's insistence on cutting the latter on moral and aesthetic grounds (so setting aside the legal implications relating to the OPA and VRA) was based around the issue of eroticising sexual violence. Carl Daft vigorously challenged the idea that *Last House* did any such thing: 'The BBFC's interpretation of *The Last House on the Left* as "erotic" would appear to be quite unique', he remarked. 'Reviewers over the years have invariably referred to the cold, flat, dispassionate style of the film-making – quite the opposite of "erotica" in fact' (cited in Kermode, 2001). This is not the place to undertake a close analysis of *Last House* and the problems it caused for the BBFC (I will return to it, briefly, in the final chapter), but it is worth noting that the case is another indicator of how blunt a tool the censor's knife can be. The cuts centred around the violence – the information on the BBFC's website refers to 'Cuts required to humiliation of woman forced to urinate, violent stabbing assault on woman and removal of her entrails, and woman's chest carved with a knife' (BBFC, 2002c). However, it may be that the more discomfiting elements of the scene are harder to pinpoint, and have more to do with the tone of the film as a whole, and in particular the relish with which the gang forces the two women to 'get it on' with one another, as the character Krug (David A. Hess) puts it. The way that this scenario crosses over into the overly familiar territory of heterosexual pornography does not require spelling out (and it is notable that neither this, nor the humiliation of forcing one of the victims to urinate is present in the parallel scene in the 2009 remake; the disembowelment is replaced by graphic footage of knife wounds to the stomach).

The hearing finally ruled in favour of the BBFC, despite the detailed challenges to its decisions presented by Carl Daft, who also pointed out discrepancies in the detail of the BBFC's judgements: three cuts totalling eighty-five seconds demanded in 1999, and four cuts totalling sixteen seconds in 2001, with only two cuts totalling five seconds consistent between the two submissions.[33] Blue Underground, forced to accept defeat, issued a cut version later in the year (*Last House* would finally be passed uncut in October 2008). In the meantime, the delay in finalising the decision over *Last House* in the summer of 2002 probably held back the announcement of any decision on *Straw Dogs*.

Straw Dogs Unleashed

The decision to pass *Straw Dogs* uncut with an '18' certificate appears to have been formalised, finally, on 1 July 2002.[34] Reports appeared in the press the following day, including in the *Guardian*, which noted that, 'The decision ... follows advice from clinical psychologists who specialise in work with sex offenders, and a focus group panel' (Travis, 2002). The release attracted a degree of press attention, including interviews with Susan George (Thomson, 2002; Campion, 2002). On 24 July 2002, a one-minute-forty-second trailer was passed uncut and granted a '15' certificate and on 21 September, Pearson Television International Inc. (of which Fremantle was a subsidiary) had their submission of the film passed with no cuts for home video, rated '18'. On 7 October, Fremantle Home Video released *Straw Dogs,* uncut, on both DVD and VHS videotape. The rush to meet the Christmas market meant that one or two authoring errors crept into the process – some typos in the pages of information on the DVD, and a delay before the beginning of the film caused by problems synchronising the video with a commentary track – but the DVD release otherwise did full justice to the film, and the hard work of all those involved in its production.

The apparent contradiction between allowing *Straw Dogs* an uncut certificate and denying *Last House* the same privilege was undoubtedly a further embarrassment. As I noted above, Whittam Smith had offered what had seemed to be a definitive position as recently as 1999, indicating that he believed the film would never be passed. In a radio interview in the same year, James Ferman had expressed satisfaction that, even if the boundaries had shifted since his retirement, the BBFC had nevertheless remained consistent in holding his firm line against attempts to certificate *Straw Dogs*. Peter Woods believes that the BBFC attempted to give their change of policy a degree of plausibility and coherence by stressing in press releases and interviews the difference between the uncut version of the film and the 'R'-rated cut in terms of reception of the rape scene. As I have already detailed, the idea that the ambiguity of the first rape was 'given context' by the second rape was crucial to their justification; its inclusion mitigated against the notion of the so-called rape myth: by including the second, more violent rape, the BBFC implied, the film countered the charge that it endorsed or eroticised sexual violence. However, as Woods pointed out in a conversation with the author about the matter, the BBFC had both versions in front of them in 1999, and had chosen to reject both. In retrospect, it is hard to see the decision to certificate *Straw Dogs* for home video uncut after eighteen years as anything but a U-turn by the BBFC.

The story of *Straw Dogs'* journey to home video in the US is much more straightforward. The 'R'-rated version was released by CBS Fox/ABC in 1992. In September 1996, Twentieth Century-Fox released *Straw Dogs* on VHS in its *edited* form in the US, and in January 1999, Anchor Bay released a DVD version in its uncut form with a running time of 118 mins, rated 'R'. In March 2003, the highly regarded Criterion Collection label prepared an edition of *Straw Dogs* with a remastered, enhanced picture, and with a number of special features and commentary tracks. The same version was released by MGM on home video in the US in October 2004.

✗ Part 3

KEY THEMES AND IDEAS

Introduction

Straw Dogs occupies a peculiar place in the canon of Sam Peckinpah's work for a number of reasons. Apart from the war film *Cross of Iron* (1976), it is the only one of his films set outside the Americas. Furthermore, of his key works – that is, discounting the pulpy thrillers *The Killer Elite* (1975) and *The Osterman Weekend* (1983), and the wretched action-comedy *Convoy* (1978) – it is almost the only film that cannot be assigned the label, more or less loosely, of 'Western'; the exceptions from the key works are *The Getaway* (1972) and, again, *Cross of Iron*. There are indeed ways in which *Straw Dogs* can be usefully interpreted, despite its English setting, as a displaced Western. I will also argue that the film is better understood as an investigation of American cultural and political anxieties at the beginning of the 1970s than it is as a depiction of rural life in a remote corner of the UK. At the time of its first theatrical release, it was the cumulative effect of the violence throughout the film, not simply the rape scene, that provoked most controversy.[35] In the years that followed, as feminist critics engaged with the film more directly and more forcefully, the sensitivities around the movie shifted to focus more specifically on what I discuss below under the heading 'The Problem of Amy'.

The discussion that follows, then, begins with what preoccupied the critics, and presumably the audiences, in 1971 and 1972: the 'mob violence' of the siege, its rootedness in certain codes of masculinity that are traceable through other Peckinpah key works, and the depiction of the clash between liberal pacifism and violent response. The second half of the discussion turns to a more detailed consideration of its representation of gender, power and sexualised violence.

Straw Dogs, Masculinity and Violence

Around the time he completed *The Wild Bunch*, Peckinpah came across the work of Robert Ardrey, a Hollywood screenwriter of the 1940s and 1950s who had become equally well known for his writings on social anthropology. In brief, Ardrey posited that the human species had to be understood as another animal, rather than as a unique kind of being superior to other living creatures. He argued that humans were naturally aggressive and territorial: according to *African Genesis*, warfare is precipitated when the 'defensive instinct of a determined territorial proprietor is challenged by the predatory compulsions of an equally determined territorial neighbour' (Ardrey, 1961, p. 173). It is not hard to see why one Swedish reviewer believed that the siege scene, in particular Sumner's proclamation that 'I will not allow violence against this house' can be heard as 'an exact echo of Ardrey' (Ruuth, 1972, p. 1). Jay Cocks also invoked Ardrey's concept of the territorial imperative in his review for *Time* magazine (SPC Cocks, 1971, p. 87). Peckinpah was certainly musing in Ardrey's intellectual shadow when he said to a *Daily Telegraph* interviewer,

> Everybody seems to deny that we're human. We're violent by nature. We're going to survive by being violent. If we don't recognise that we're violent people, we're dead. We're going to be on some beach, and we're going to drop bombs on each other. I would like to understand the nature of violence. Is there a way to channel it, to use it positively?
> (SPC Yergin, 1971, p. 38)

Peckinpah's interest in codes of masculinity, including male comradeship, conflict and territorial struggle, had been noted and discussed as key themes in his earlier Westerns, but took on a new sense of definition in the light of the discoveries he was making via Ardrey.

It is not difficult to read *Straw Dogs* as a displaced Western: the village pub is a clear analogue for the archetypal saloon setting, allowing for encounters between the protagonist and antagonist, or between the outsider and insider figures, in a public but enclosed space. In the opening scene, David's sneakers and preppy slacks and sweater are markers of his fish-out-of-water status: customary uniform in his home environment of well-heeled transatlantic academia it may be; here, in a world of tweed, Wellington boots and flat caps, he looks merely vulnerable and slightly ridiculous. David's request for 'any American cigarettes' seems to go unheeded, and as he waits, awkward and a little nervous, he becomes a witness to a display of macho posturing. The dispute over Tom's extra pint certainly establishes a good deal about power and status within the village. David, evidently embarrassed at having been knocked around the room, turns away from the violence in a way that gives the audience an early insight into his pacifism. A rehearsal note, ticked approvingly by Peckinpah, remarks that 'Bertie is pushed into David to see how he would react, to provoke him into showing them how tough he is' (SPC Anon, 1971c, p. 2). One might also read the scene as Tom sublimating the violence he would like to direct against the American into his row with the landlord instead; the triumphant raising aloft of his pint is an almost feral strut of power on display, one that seems to provoke Major Scott into intervening, finally and reluctantly. The camera cuts, in Western mode, from a

Screen capture: Major Scott, the broken arm of the law.

close-up of Harry (Robert Keegan), his beard wet from a gulped pint, to a silent, watchful figure in the corner: Major Scott, unamused, unimpressed, almost (but not quite) impassive: a note from a meeting about the pub scenes remarks, 'Scott to totally ignore Tom Hedden but be totally aware of him. Note antagonism' (SPC Anon, 1971c). As he quietly confronts Tom Hedden over the disputed pint, his tone is authoritative and a little sour; patronising, with the slightest edge of aggression. This time, at least, Hedden has to cede to the power of the law and he leaves, taking his men with him.

These characters – Venner, Scutt, Cawsey, Riddaway (Donald Webster), Tom Hedden (a group occasionally augmented by Bertie Hedden) – are most often seen together, and they constitute the vigilante posse in the final farmhouse siege. The two publicity shots reproduced below show how close the parallels are with the Western tradition. The masculine zone is demarcated by their discourse, too, in particular the sly hints of bestiality in the quips and drinking songs that pepper the early scenes, and their

Publicity still: *The Wild Bunch*.

observation of and interaction with Amy, whom they metaphorically (and, if we remember the exchange between Scutt and Cawsey over the underwear stolen from her bedroom, quite literally) sniff around like animals in heat. The latent homoeroticism that remains was toned down considerably from early drafts that included miming of anal sex following discussion of Amy's sexual past with Venner (SPC Goodman, 1970a, p. 7), and references to the men riding in the truck, grabbing each other 'by the groin' and 'rubbing each other's privates' (the latter removed at Baum's insistence [SPC Melnick, 1970b: 5]).

They treat David with contempt masked by a mock deference: all the men call him 'Mr. Sumner' or 'sir'; Cawsey's forelock-tugging in particular is comically sardonic. Later, en route to the village pub, the workmen deliberately force David's car off the road with their truck, but he perseveres with his lonely trip to the pub all the same. When Major Scott tells him he was just about to

Publicity still: *Straw Dogs*.

call up to the farm to welcome him into 'our little community', David casts a sidelong glance at the men and remarks, 'I've just been welcomed.' As he leaves with the Major, he pays for his drink, pauses and then throws down a few more banknotes. 'Buy 'em all one,' he says. It's presumably intended as a reconciliatory gesture, but only comes across as condescending and further evidence to the villagers of the way in which the American, unwittingly or not, lords it over them. Moments later, as he leaves with Scott, they all pointedly bid the magistrate goodnight, saying nothing to Sumner.

David's eagerness to establish some kind of common ground with the villagers continues, despite their rebuffs. When Amy pushes him to confront the men over the death of her pet cat, he repeatedly defers confrontation (he tells Amy he's waiting for a moment to 'catch them off guard'); first, he shares his cigarettes with them, and then he invites them in. As they stand drinking his beer, with Amy watching and waiting for that moment to come (more in hope than expectation), the villagers offer to take him shooting with them; pleased and flattered, Sumner readily agrees. If the text suggests he is forging some kind of bond – he dismisses Amy's objection, and raises his glass to seal the deal – the subtext tells a different story: the editing repeatedly cuts between the group of men, with Scutt eyeing Amy; Amy herself (seated uncomfortably, staring at David); and David, metaphorically and physically backed into a corner, against the grandfather clock (the same corner Amy is backed into by Venner just prior to the rape) (see screen capture, opposite).

Amy grows more and more contemptuous of David, appalled by his failure to cope with any kind of confrontation. Just as the villagers scorn him for his failure to match up to their notions of masculine behaviour, Amy attacks him in a similar vein: 'if you could hammer a nail, Venner and Scutt wouldn't be here', she snaps. However, she is much more deeply dismayed by David's refusal to consider the implications of the killing of the cat. For Amy, it is either Scutt or Cawsey proving the point that they could 'get into your bedroom'. David stares, then shakes his head: 'I don't believe that.' His wilful blindness sets him up for ridicule when they abandon him on the moor but, far more seriously, leaves Amy vulnerable and exposed. It is not until David's

Screen capture: Cornered.

liberal principles are challenged that he finally squares up to confrontation. The prospect of handing over an injured and seemingly defenceless innocent to a vigilante mob brings David face to face with the logical end of pacifism. Once he chooses to meet force with force, his transformation is complete and terrifying, and to explore it fully, I need to put it in the context of something I have already referred to (see pp. 21–3): the Vietnam War.

Straw Dogs and Vietnam

> *I just started killing in any kinda way I can kill. It just came. I didn't know I had it in me. … My whole mind just went. It just went. And after you start it's very easy to keep on. The hardest is to kill the first time but once you kill, then it becomes easier to kill the next person and the next one and the next one. Because I had no feelings, no emotions. Nothing.*
>
> (Vietnam Veteran Private First Class Varnado Simpson, Charlie Company [Bilton and Sim, 1992, p. 130])

On the morning of 16 March 1968, members of Charlie Company, 1st Battalion, 20th Infantry Regiment, US Army 11th Brigade, moved in on a hamlet called Tu Cung in squads, shooting anything that moved and tossing grenades into bunkers and dwellings. By the end of the day, the place that the US Army had labelled My Lai 4 on their maps would be a pitiful scene of utter devastation. Lt. William Calley had overseen the deaths of over 500 old men, women and children, shot, stabbed or blown to pieces. Villagers had been lined up in front of irrigation ditches and mown down in mass executions. A number of women had been raped. Some victims had been bayoneted, cut open and mutilated; others shot in the back of the head whilst praying. A baby was shot in the face as its frantic mother cradled it in her arms. Calley himself, mid-interrogation, picked up a two-year-old child that had crawled out of a ditch, shoved it back down the slope and shot it dead, before calmly returning to the monk he had been questioning.

What came to be known as the My Lai Massacre was covered up by the army for over a year; they initially reported the incident as a US victory resulting in the deaths of over 100 Vietcong. The real story finally broke in November 1969 with extensive coverage in *Time, Newsweek, Life* and on CBS television. In the immediate wake of the revelations, if only for a brief period, the effect on the American national conscience was profound. It was not long before the impact dissipated in the wake of a series of careful moves by the army to censor reports on the Massacre, and of increasingly desperate attempts by the Nixon government to resist the tide of public opinion turning against the war. Nevertheless, it remained a jarring wake-up call for many who had become inured to the footage from the frontline screened on the nightly news. Considered again forty years on, time and distance having given a context for this appalling war crime, it is undeniable that it has been a major factor in reassessments of the United States' shameful legacy in Southeast Asia. When US Marines went on the rampage in the Iraqi town of Haditha in November 2005, slaughtering twenty-four men, women and children (all civilians), My Lai was a familiar reference point. Veteran reporter Jon Swain compared the stories circulating about Haditha – a Marine urinating on one of the victims, others chasing each other around the rooms wielding body parts – with what he had witnessed himself in Vietnam, where troops posed for photographs in front of piles of corpses and made necklaces of ears cut from dead Vietcong soldiers (Swain, 2008, p. 7).

For Peckinpah, working on *Straw Dogs* at the time that Lt. Calley was found guilty of the murder of twenty-two civilians, the My Lai Massacre 'emblemized', in Stephen Prince's words, 'the brutality and corruption of the Vietnam War and of the society that was waging it' (Prince, 1998, p. 35). Prince quotes a telegram Peckinpah sent to Nixon urging the President not to free Calley, and to press for a fuller investigation of exactly who was responsible for the Massacre (Calley would be freed in 1974, after several reductions in his original sentence). Prince also shows how Peckinpah would often return to the theme of My Lai in defence of the representation of violence in his own films (Prince, 1998, pp. 35–7). Two years after My Lai, in May 1970, national guardsmen opened fire on a student anti-war demonstration at Kent State University, Ohio, killing four and wounding nine. The tragedy provoked further protests and a nationwide student strike.

The aftermath of My Lai was, for Peckinpah, a display of government corruption and cowardly abdication of responsibility – something that would be obvious preoccupations in his later films such as *The Killer Elite* and *The Osterman Weekend*. However, more significant for our purposes were the questions that the inhuman brutality of 16 March 1968 begged about man's capacity for violence and cruelty. The My Lai Massacre may have been on Peckinpah's mind specifically when he commented in an interview for *Rolling Stone*:

> It's about the violence within all of us … . The violence which is reflecting on the political condition of the world today. It serves a dual purpose, I intended it to have a cathartic affect [sic]. Someone may feel a strange, sick exultation at the violence, but he should ask himself, 'What is going on in my heart?' I wanted to achieve a catharsis through pity and fear. (SPC Hodenfield, 1971, p. 12).

Screen capture: Sumner the conscientious objector: AMP poster.

The Vietnam references in the film are subtle – younger audiences today with no knowledge of the historical context can miss them completely – but they would have seemed more overt in 1971. Highly visible at the end of one of the arguments between David and Amy, on the left side of the blackboard, is a peace poster, a naively stylised painting of a flower on a yellow background, emblazoned with childlike handwriting that reads, 'War is not healthy for children and other living things.'[36] Early drafts of the script placed a much heavier emphasis on the reasons behind David's decision to leave the US and spend his sabbatical period in a remote village in Cornwall, in his wife's former family home. One version of the argument finds her yelling at him, 'It's an age of confrontation [but] you run away … first from the things in the States … and now from the things here' (SPC G&P, 1970j, unpaginated).

The final version of the scene as shot is both less explicit in these terms, and at the same time more subtly powerful: the way in which David and Amy carefully step around the metaphorical wounded elephant in the living room gives a good impression of how much remains unarticulated between them, and is indicative of their inability to communicate effectively with one another. David's insistence that 'I was involved with my work' cuts little ice with Amy: as far as she is concerned, they have ended up in England because, for him, 'there was no place left to hide'. David defuses the dispute, simultaneously trying to save face by changing the subject: 'We're here because you once said you thought we could be happier here, remember?' It's a characteristically sly counter that puts Amy back on the defensive, retreating into an apology that David manipulates still further ('Are you sorry sorry, or just sorry?'… 'Sorry sorry', she replies).

What David is hiding from is the prospect of, in Amy's words, the need to 'take a stand … to commit'. His response to Amy's challenge is that 'I never claimed to be one of the involved' (earlier drafts included more explicit references to 'chicken shit radicals blowing up banks and schools' [SPC G&P, 1970h, p. 38; SPC G&P, 1971b, p. 45]). For Peckinpah, this is one of the bitterest ironies of David's character: a typewritten script note muses, 'it is precisely men like David who are leaving the United States who are the only ones who can "save" it' (SPC Anon, 1971a).[37] Although the conversation between Amy and David as shot contained less specific references to civil unrest in America, there is a short exchange between David, Scutt and Cawsey that reminds us of the context for this narrative: Cawsey reels off a casual list of violent incidents – 'Bombing, rioting, sniping; shooting the blacks' and Scutt cuts in, 'Was you involved in it, sir? I mean, did you take part?', and Cawsey almost overlaps: 'See anybody get knifed?' After a pause so well timed one might be tempted to attribute it to Pinter himself, Sumner replies, 'Just between commercials.' His steady gaze indicates that the conversation is over.

It could be argued that the one of the movie's key premises is something of a Vietnam metaphor: the civilised American parachuted into an alien society, defending a helpless native against marauding forces. Certainly David claims the farmhouse as his own territory in the final showdown, insisting 'this is where I live. This is me. I will not allow violence against this house.'[38] With all choices eliminated except to fight or die, Sumner sets about his defence of the house (the Western homestead) in a ruthlessly methodical fashion.

A Man's House Is …

There is a sharp irony in what finally provokes Sumner into action: it is not the contempt with which he has been treated; it is not the attack on his household that is the wider signification of the killing of the pet cat; and it is not the rape of his wife, which he knows nothing about. The terrible violence that is unleashed on him, Amy and the farmhouse is instigated by his determination to defend the man he has accidentally knocked down on the way home, a man who has – also accidentally – killed Janice Hedden. If we want to understand the thinking behind Peckinpah's identification of David as the 'heavy' rather than the hero of the movie, we need to start with this fundamental misstep. Whether or not we admire him for defending Henry Niles on principle, the fact that he has once again demonstrated his stubborn single-mindedness from a position of ignorance and error is of a piece with the arrogance and pig-headedness that is at the root of so many of the problems he has created for himself and his wife.

The vigilante posse emerges from the fog, already fired up on booze and righteous indignation. Tom steps down from the truck loading his shotgun, and Venner at first tries to defuse the situation by sending in a delegation – himself, Scutt and Cawsey – but physical violence ensues within moments. Cawsey starts slapping Niles to rouse him, and David pulls him off. However, when he tries to stop Scutt attacking the injured man, Scutt responds violently, throwing David back across the room. This is a showdown, and the two men circle one another, Scutt threatening, David trying to contain a rising sense of panic. Sumner continues to try and triumph with logic and reason over the villagers' threats and demands, but his insistence that Niles is his responsibility is met with ridicule: 'Your responsibility?' Scutt mocks; 'Why?', to which David has no answer, instead retreating into a territorial imperative. 'This is *my* house', he insists (and at that precise moment Peckinpah cuts away to a fleeting shot of Tom outside readying his weapon). Only when Amy intervenes and bluffs that the police will be arriving soon do the villagers back down.

As the heat rises, David slips from a show of confidence (there is a wonderful moment as he draws a heavy curtain across the doorway, assuring Amy, 'I can *handle* this' with a wan smile, just as the curtain becomes stuck on its rail), to a growing sense of nervousness as the violence rapidly escalates. At first, even after Cawsey throws the first brick through a window, David continues to try and reason with them, threatening to press charges, offering them 'one more chance' – or otherwise 'there will be *real* trouble'. When a moment of silence follows, he winks reassuringly and patronisingly at Amy, but almost immediately the smashing of glass resumes around the house. A turning point comes when David realises that Amy is not on his side – when she insists they hand Niles over, David objects, 'they'll beat him to death'. Amy replies that she doesn't care, and this seems to be a revelation to David: 'You really don't care, do you?' he marvels, appalled. For a moment, he seems to hover indecisively, then he turns back to her: 'No. I care. This is where I live. This is me. I will not allow violence against this house. No way.' Moments later, the Major arrives, to David's great relief. In the Western paradigm, Scott is the sheriff ('you're the law here', David reminds him), and when his confrontation with Tom Hedden results in his death after a struggle over Hedden's shotgun, the last chance to avoid further violence is lost.

The impact on David is profound and immediate. The audience watches he and Amy watching the Major die, and as they turn from the window the camera crash-zooms out to convey their sense of shock and terror. David shifts gear, preparing himself to repel the assault, and his tactics are militarily precise: he strategically arranges the lighting, wires the windows, prepares boiling oil on the stove and lays the mantrap.[39] He is by this point utterly focused on resisting the siege, and is brutal in his treatment of Amy, slapping her and pulling her away from the door by the hair when she tries to let Venner in (an attack which inevitably recalls Venner's dragging of Amy by the hair in the rape scene). As the attack enters its last phase, with the villagers finally managing to force their way into the house, David cues up deafening bagpipe music, and it provides a strident, martial aural backdrop for the combat that follows, from which David emerges triumphant – if the sick despair he feels as he surveys the devastation around him can be called that. 'Jesus,' he gasps. 'I killed 'em all.'

At least one of the other endings considered for the film (see pp. 15–16) would have undoubtedly been bleaker than the final cut, but it is hard to imagine anything more finely balanced than the one Peckinpah chose. David's reply to Niles's vulnerable 'I don't know my way home' – 'That's OK. I don't either' – is a wonderfully eloquent expression of everything he has had to surrender – his liberal convictions, his pacifism – and of everything he has discovered about himself – his capacity for violence, and the ingenuity and ruthlessness with which he is able dispatch his opponents. For David, like so many who returned, haunted, from the Vietnam conflict, there is no way home to the man he thought he was.

The Problem of Amy

If it was violence that provoked the initial heated debate over *Straw Dogs*, it was the film's representation of sexual violence that would shape its troubled reputation in years to come. It has to be said that Peckinpah would on occasion mischievously court such controversy: in 1974, prompted by an interviewer that 'There is a whole Peckinpah line now of ladies who believe that if they get raped, they'll get into it,' Peckinpah replied, 'Most women do'; 'I think there's probably a difference of opinion on that,' came the retort: 'Not from women,' Peckinpah replied (Bryson, 1974, p. 141). Even more notorious is an interview granted to *Playboy* magazine in August 1972, a few months after *Straw Dogs* was released. From the outset, it is clear that Peckinpah feels no compulsion to offer reasoned, responsible replies to the questions put to him by William Murray, and his mood varies from playful, to confessional, to aggressive over the course of the interview. He is self-deprecating ('I'm looking for a job. I'm a whore. I go where I'm kicked'), and defensive about *Straw Dogs*, particularly in relation to the quality of the source material: 'Read the goddamn book. You'll die gagging in your own vomit' (Murray, 1972,

p. 101). However, it is his remarks on the character of Amy in particular which have been most closely pored over.

I have already noted Pauline Kael's 'fascist work of art' review and Peckinpah's response (see pp. 37–8), and he was clearly still smarting from that when Murray interviewed him: 'I like Kael', he confessed; 'she's a feisty little gal and I enjoy drinking with her – which I have done on occasion – but here', he continued, with reference to the 'fascist' label, 'she's cracking walnuts with her ass.' Musing on the rape scene in *Straw Dogs*, he exclaims, 'Doesn't Kael know *anything* about sex? Dominating and being dominated: the fantasy, too, of being taken by force is certainly one way people make love' (Murray, 1972, p. 100). The gulf that separates the realm of sexual fantasy from actual sexual assault, of course, is the gap that Peckinpah, consciously or not, is eliding here. A number of critics have argued that his mischief-making contributed to the storm clouds of controversy that have gathered around *Straw Dogs* (see, for example, Prince, 1998, pp. 126–7), and claimed that those clouds obscure the film's meanings, and its representation of gender, power and sexuality. My own view is that an understanding of the film and a reading of a range of interpretations should be informed by a multitude of factors, including an awareness of the extent to which Peckinpah at times would 'perform' the role of misogynist in order to provoke. However, it is impossible to ignore the construction of Amy that Peckinpah offered publicly, and shaped in scripts, notes and exchanges with colleagues, and these elements also require scrutiny.

His reflections upon the character of Amy are unequivocally condemnatory: he describes her as 'a young, uninformed, bitchy, hot-bodied little girl who hasn't grown up yet' in the *Playboy* interview (Murray, 1972, p. 100). A little later in the same interview, he comes out with one of his most infamous remarks: 'There are two kinds of women. There are women, and then there's pussy. ... Amy is pussy, under the veneer of being a woman' (p. 104). Peckinpah's conceptualisation of 'pussy' is hard to pin down, but he seems to define her in contradistinction to a 'woman' (or 'a good woman'), whom he sees as 'a partner'; by contrast, 'pussy' seems to be 'a smart unscrupulous cunt [who] can always use her looks to get some poor slob to marry her'; Amy 'is basically pussy', Peckinpah concludes, and Sumner 'obviously married the wrong dame' (p. 105). If such a judgement – and its embodiment in the character of Amy on screen – seems offensive, Peckinpah can scarcely shift the blame to the source novel. By his own admission, the only thing he and Goodman retrieved from what he calls 'this rotten book' was 'the siege itself' (p. 101); as noted previously, there is no rape in Williams's novel, and the sexual dynamic between the couple is also markedly different, with an emphasis on George's impotence (which is miraculously remedied at the end of the book by his violent response to the siege). Gordon Williams, the author of the novel in question, claimed recently that the rape scene appeared in the movie because 'Peckinpah "liked to abuse women in his films"' (Williams, 2003b).

It is undeniable that there is a measure of misogyny in Peckinpah's comments on the character of Amy, and his associated generalisations about women. However, while taking into account Peckinpah's tendency to enjoy the role of *provocateur*, we must also acknowledge that the remarks would have been less shocking in the early 1970s than they sound today. The early press reviews, the majority of them written by men, betray a brand of chauvinism that was still par for the course in 1971; there was a routine acceptance amongst male reporters and critics that Amy was 'asking for it': *Rolling Stone* magazine, in a summary of the action, notes that Amy 'gets raped by some local mugs, and enjoys it …' (SPC Hodenfield, 1971, p. 12); William Murray, summing up the film's narrative, claims Amy 'teases their lust and is eventually the rather willing victim of a double rape' (Murray, 1972, p. 97). For *Newsweek*, Paul D. Zimmerman made an interesting connection with *Lady Chatterley's Lover*, remarking that,

> The workmen seem to leap from the pages of D. H. Lawrence, pastoral proletarians led by their libidos. And the lady of the house might be Connie Chatterley, half-yearning to be raped, parading before them braless and, sometimes, sweaterless.

He was also moved to herald the rape scene quite unashamedly as 'a masterful piece of erotic cinema, a flawless acting out of the female fantasy of absolute violation' (SPC Zimmerman, 1971, p. 87). Other major press reviews, including the *New York Times*, *San Francisco Chronicle* and *Time* magazine (see p. 38) offered analogous descriptions.

To these critics, Pauline Kael laid down a gauntlet early, describing Amy as a 'Lolita-wife …a sex kitten … an unsatisfied little tart …'; the rape scene, she claimed, 'says that women really want the rough stuff, that deep down they're little beasts asking to be made submissive' (Kael, 1972, p. 80). Molly Haskell was even more aggressive, furious at the way in which the film seemed to her to endorse the 'saying no but meaning yes' rape myth, and interpreting it as a typical male response to the 'threat' of feminism:

> The closer women come to claiming their rights and achieving independence in real life, the more loudly and stridently films tell us it's a man's world. … As Susan George, in *Straw Dogs*, struts around like Daisy Mae before the brier-patch yokels, and then gets it once, twice, and again, for the little tease she is. The provocative, sex-obsessed bitch is one of the great male-chauvinist (and, apparently, territorialist) fantasies, along with the fantasy that she is constantly fantasizing rape. (Haskell, 1974, p. 363)

Stephen Farber, one of the few male critics to take issue with the film's gender politics at the time, noted with concern that both Amy and Janice are 'teases', and that 'Peckinpah holds them responsible for capriciously inciting violence that they cannot control' (Farber, 1972b, p. 5), and later generations of feminist critics have been even more scathing: Carol Clover sees the rape in the film as 'a classic in the "asking for it" tradition' (Clover, 1992, p. 139), and Linda Ruth Williams suggests that, 'In *Straw Dogs* … femininity *is* perversity, and women can *only* misbehave' (Williams, 1995, pp. 26–7). What is it about the representation of Amy that has so angered these critics? A closer look at the script development, and at the representation of sex and gender in the film more generally, will reveal more about Peckinpah's approach to the problem of

Amy, and help define the parameters of the debate before a close analysis of
the rape scene itself.

Amy's first appearance in the film, moments after the end of the
opening-credits sequence, is an obvious first point of reference. What we
could term the 'Amy establishing shot' is a close-up of her from the waist to
just below her shoulders, focused on her breasts, braless, under a clinging
white sweater. It is a shot that has been much discussed by critics since, for
obvious reasons. Her sartorial choice is something that will become a point of
contention between her and David later in the film, when his increased
anxiety about the apparent fragility of his ownership over her begins to bite.
Linda Ruth Williams describes the shot as 'almost parodic' in its evocation of
'fragmented femininity' (Williams, 1995, p. 27). The focus on Amy's sexuality
from the very opening moment is rooted in the earliest drafts of the script:
Goodman's first version includes the line 'a short leather jacket over a sweater
fails to hide the outline of her perfect breasts' (SPC Goodman, 1970a, p. 1);
and Peckinpah's first rewrite – 'the nipples hard against the cold – firmly
outlined against the thin jersey of her blouse' – provides an accurate
description of what was shot, minus the 'leather vest' (SPC G&P, 1970a, p. 2).

Screen capture: The Amy 'establishing shot'.

The camera tilts up to focus on Amy's apparently guileless face. In doing so, it establishes the mystery at the heart of her character – her varying levels of awareness about her sexual magnetism, how far she is willing to use it to her own ends, and how much or little control she can exert over the men that are drawn in by it. Amy is constructed as a confusing amalgam of cunning and innocence, sending out conflicted signals. Her first action in the film encapsulates the enigma: she smiles, and the camera cuts from her face to Charlie Venner emerging from the telephone box with a look of amazement and recognition, to David approaching from the other direction, carrying a box full of groceries. It is (presumably deliberately) unclear whether Amy is smiling at her husband or her former boyfriend. Meanwhile, Janice Hedden is depicted walking behind her, helping her cousin Bobby to carry (appropriately) a mantrap. Janice is evidently scrutinising Amy's swaying gait with care, imitating her in a fashion that is as studied as Amy's seems natural. The emphasis is clear even in the first draft script ('She is one of those extremely feminine women who emit a constant measure of sexuality no matter what they are doing' [SPC Goodman, 1970a, p. 1]), and Peckinpah's first rewrite elaborates in some detail:

> AS SHE MOVES you become conscious that there is a quiet motor running. It's the kind you don't hear often, it's one that you listen to out of the corner of your eyes and out of the corner of your desire … and the heart of the motor is between her lovely legs. She is wild and she is sweet. She is almost everything that anybody in Wakely ever dreamed of. (SPC G&P, 1970a, p. 2)

The voyeuristic tone of this description is in keeping with that of the *Playboy* interview, and a letter from Goodman to Peckinpah confirms that the words are all Sam's [SPC Goodman, 1970b, p. 2]).

The opening scene is crucial to our understanding of the issue of 'ownership' over Amy. When Amy, observing Henry Niles, asks Charlie why Niles has not been 'put away', Charlie replies, 'Oh, we can take care of our own

Significantly, when David asks about Venner as he and Amy drive home, she laughingly dismisses it; her line – 'By the way, Venner did try and get fresh once. Nothing happened' – is bitterly ironic in retrospect. After David and Amy have returned to the farmhouse, the rat-catcher Chris Cawsey reveals to Norman Scutt what he has stolen from the bedroom: a pair of Amy's knickers. 'You like my trophy?' he asks him. 'Bugger your trophy', replies Scutt; 'I want what was in 'em.' In feminist terms, the way in which Amy is being objectified in this scene is evident from the use of pronouns: 'You gonna have a crack at her, Norman?' asks Cawsey; Scutt's reply is an early warning of the violence skulking beneath the surface: 'No, ten months inside is enough for me.' Cawsey muses, 'I could do with some of *that*, too, Normie. Charlie Venner – he had some of *it*. Years ago. When she was here with her father' [my emphasis]. The aggressive male competitiveness that erupts repeatedly makes an early appearance when Scutt comes back with a snarling rejoinder, 'Venner's a bloody liar. And so are you.' Soon afterwards, the knickers make a second appearance in the pub, offering up Amy (or at least, the prospect of her) to wider public consumption. The film cuts from David and Amy making love to Cawsey throwing the panties to Scutt, who proceeds to taunt Charlie with them, before stuffing them down his own shirt (and from here the film cuts straight to Amy and David arguing the following morning).

How does Amy understand her own status in relation to the men that encircle her? An undated and anonymous script note refers to Amy 'returning "home" to preen', and soon finding that 'the preening does not suffice emotionally' (SPC Anon, 1971a). The opening scene includes a carefully blocked conversation between Amy, David and Venner that raises questions about who belongs to whom. Despite her assertion to the contrary when they argue over it later, it is Amy who suggests that Charlie might be willing to help fix the roof of the garage at the farm (earlier drafts had David extending the invitation [SPC G&P, 1970a, p. 5]). David, somewhat caught off guard and perhaps unwilling to seem rude, accepts the invitation. Amy meanwhile stands alongside her former boyfriend, bowing her head out of amusement at

Screen capture: Taking sides.

Janice's attempt to elbow her way into the conversation, and then looking up rather shyly from beneath her fringe at David. The grouping of the actors is perfectly framed here: Janice in the background, thrusting out her chest in the vain hope that David might notice her; David on the lefthand side of the screen, and Amy and Charlie positioned as a partnered couple to the right, as the negotiation over working on the barn continues. David soon retreats to the pub in search of cigarettes; a script-meeting note remarks that his decision to run one more errand 'is the first evidence of David's ability to walk away from situations he is unable to cope with' (SPC Anon, 1971b, p. 1). Peckinpah's astute framing of this sequence also anticipates Amy's shift of loyalties at the climax of the farmhouse siege. Meanwhile, the edginess of the David/Charlie relationship is already being established. However we might choose to interpret Amy's negotiation of her position in the scene, it is hard to avoid the sense that she is sending conflicting signals about her loyalties in relation to her new husband, and her old acquaintances in the village.

   Early drafts of the script suggest a backstory that has matched a stuffy academic with a young trophy wife[40] – Amy, expressing her feelings of the stairs. However, the 'woman' lines, when they are first added to the screenplay, are far more assertive and emphatic than they are in the shooting script, written as, 'I – am – neither!! … I – am – a woman!' (SPC G&P, 1970f, p. 41): here, the punctuation of the line strongly suggests angry rebellion. However, with Amy's lines excised (and, again, they may have been cut because they seemed overly literal), the precise motivation for her strip and her glance at Venner and the others is rendered obscure. As Prince notes in his commentary, her facial expression is difficult to read (even more so than when she met the men's gaze as she steps out of the car in the preceding scene). However, for many – for some critics, for the students I discuss the film with year by year – the favoured interpretation is that it is not an act of rebellion at all, but an invitation to the men, coming from a frustrated woman who finds her own husband inadequate to satisfy her needs. It is this kind of reading that has dominated interpretation of Amy's character, particularly by feminist critics, and has inevitably impacted upon critical reception of the rape scene, which I analyse in detail in the following section.

✖ PART 4

KEY SCENE ANALYSIS

The Rape Scene: Introduction

The sequence begins as David heads out to the moors with the village workmen on the hunt. Peckinpah deftly intercuts the rape scene with David's adventure on the moor throughout the sequence; he also incorporates what he termed 'flash cuts' of David and Amy's lovemaking scene from earlier in the film in order to add layers of irony to the sequence, and to allow an insight into Amy's emotional and mental state. As I have already indicated, it is this particular scene that has proven most enduringly controversial. The long-dominant view has been that it implies an endorsement of the male rape myth that a woman who says no may really mean yes. Several critics who have offered major in-depth studies of Peckinpah's work, including Stephen Prince (1998) and Bernard Dukore (1999), mitigate the accusations of misogyny by insisting that the film as a whole, and the rape scene in particular, are structured around Amy's experience, and allow us access to her agonising ordeal. The same position is maintained by Prince in his commentary for the Criterion Collection edition of *Straw Dogs* on DVD and by Garner Simmons, David Weddle and Paul Seydor on the UK Fremantle DVD commentary. In earlier sections, I have considered the circumstances surrounding the shooting of the scene, and Susan George's experience on the set. I have also discussed the censorship of the scene in the US and the UK, both in terms of 'self-censorship' and by the MPAA and the BBFC. The analysis that follows offers a close reading of the scene itself, in its final incarnation for UK theatrical release (the idea of a 'preferred' version will be discussed in due course; see p. 114–15). After a summary of the structure of the sequences, I will consider the scene in some detail in the light of the two dominant critical readings – those accusing it of endorsing the male rape myth

(Williams, Haskell), and those who argue that the scene is defensible on the grounds that it tries to put the viewer in the position of the victim. The chapter concludes with reflections on the scene as a whole, and its significance in the *Straw Dogs* controversies.

Venner's Arrival

The scene begins with a master shot of Amy sitting in her dressing gown on a sofa in the farmhouse living room, reading a magazine. The tension that will mount over the next couple of minutes is initiated at once by Amy's hesitation on hearing the knock at the door before rising to answer it. As the door opens, the over-the-shoulder shot of Amy gives us Venner's perspective: the shot/reverse-shot emphasises the difference between them in terms of height and build and serves to accentuate Amy's vulnerability; her view of him, correspondingly, finds him dominant, filling the space of the doorway, one hand on the lintel. Amy's first thought is of David, and she asks if he is all right; Charlie's reply is breezy ('He's fine – enjoying himself'), and Amy, after another moment's hesitation, invites Charlie in, crossing to the cabinet to pour him a drink, while he puts down his gun and his bag, and then removes his coat, in easy movements that imply he is already making himself very much at home. His offer to leave is at odds with his physical attitude, and is unnerving for the audience; it reminds us that his presence here is illicit and potentially dangerous. Amy, however, apparently self-confident and seeing an opportunity to discover more about the fate of the family pet, invites him to stay and finish his drink. Her face is neutral, edging on confrontational, as she adds, 'I'd like to know what you think of cats.' The tension is palpable, and Charlie capitalises on it when he responds with an innuendo-laden retort – 'I do fancy cats' – which he uses as a cue to move in to kiss her.

Amy's first response to the kiss seems ambivalent; she neither avoids him nor struggles to escape the embrace immediately; in fact, she tilts her face towards him as he bends down to kiss her, although her ambivalence is still legible in the way she holds herself back. However, her 'Please leave me' seems to lack force – whether through fear or uncertain conviction. When he replies 'No' and moves in for a second kiss, however, she does resist, and struggles against his embrace, then shouts, 'Get out!' and slaps him across the cheek. The violence of what follows is accentuated by Peckinpah's use of slow-motion; there is a brief moment of stasis, the camera framing the two of them in a tense mid-shot, before Amy attempts to cross past him. Venner seizes her by the lapels of her gown, his face screwing into a scowl, and strikes her a blow across the face. As we hear the slap, we cut from our perspective of Venner and the back of Amy's head to a medium close-up of Amy, crying out and falling away from him across the back of the sofa. Her sobbing is heard over a rising, dissonant soundtrack, and the slow-motion effect emphasises the impact of the blow. Venner follows up by stretching out an almost immediate, apologetic hand, and Amy backs away from him, into the corner of the room, next to the grandfather clock that had been David's refuge point in the earlier scene with the workmen (see p. 79). If the balance of power seems to hover for a moment ('Don't tease me, Amy… please'), it is only fleeting. For Venner, having struck his first blow, it is simply a matter of whether he will have his way with her consent or by force. Now the camera switches between close-ups of the two of them. As he reaches out to a visibly terrified Amy, she bats away his hand and slaps him again. She attempts once more to walk swiftly past him, but he grabs her by the hair and drags her around to the sofa – the close-up on Amy's anguished face offers no respite from the brutality, and the decision to cast Venner's actions in caveman mode, seen most clearly in a fleetingly glimpsed overhead camera shot, draws attention to the troubling sexual politics of the scene. It may also owe a debt to Ardrey, with the connotations of the human animal and his atavistic urges. Another slap from Charlie mirrors the first – with another fleeting slow-motion sequence – and the editing picks up the pace sharply as Venner tears her gown and throws her onto the sofa. The confusing blur of different angles

Screen capture: Atavistic violence.

and camera set-ups may be understood as an expression of Amy's disorientation and panic.

The First Rape

Peckinpah is often acknowledged, even by his detractors, as a master of complex, fast-cut editing, and nowhere is this more evident than during the sequence that follows. A sheaf of papers in the archive has a number of detailed notes on the flash cuts and edits, in particular the sequence of shots intermingling Amy and Venner, Amy having sex with David and David out on the moor (SPC Peckinpah, 1971a, pp. 4–5). In between a number of medium-range master shots of Charlie and Amy on the sofa, Peckinpah inserts a series of images, often only a few frames and so almost subliminal in their impact, that intensifies and complicates this notorious scene. There are moments when we see precisely what Amy sees: Charlie's face looming towards her (distorted, as Stephen Prince notes, by the use of a wide-angle lens),[41] matched against a close-up view of her face framed by Charlie's hands – Venner's own point-of-view shot. As he undresses her, we get a series of these sequences, including one where a view of Charlie above her removing his sweater is matched to a shot from Amy's lovemaking with David that we saw earlier, when he removed his shirt – again, we are placed, fleetingly, inside Amy's consciousness. These moments are genuinely unsettling – Peckinpah achieves something similar when he inserts flash cuts from the rape into the church social scene to convey the sense of Amy reliving her ordeal. The sequence is complicated further by the inclusion of a flash cut of David out on the moor (and longer sequences are intercut through the scene), and this is itself juxtaposed with a Venner point-of-view shot, a close-up of Amy's breasts. When Amy tries to protest ('No, please, Charlie'), he is firm, and when she makes a move to try to get up from beneath him, he raises his hand threateningly. 'I don't want to reave you, but I will,' he warns her.[42]

Much of the next couple of minutes is shot in long and medium range, with the master shots displaying and emphasising Susan George's naked form. At one point, Amy attempts to cover her breasts, and Charlie tears her arms away. As the rape continues, Peckinpah uses tighter, head-and-shoulder shots, with some longer cutaways to David on the moor, as well as more of his characteristic, fleeting flash cuts. But what we should be making of the rape itself is now becoming more confusing; Amy's pants and gasps no longer seem like struggles to resist, but more like signs of pleasure, and the expression on her face might just as easily be orgasmic as agonised. After a clever panning shot conveying the sense of Amy's gaze moving from a focus on the fireplace up and across to Charlie, up his shoulder to his face, the sequence moves into a tighter framing on the two of them, with more head-and-shoulder close-ups. Amy now stretches up to touch Charlie's face, with one sigh of a word, 'Easy.' Reaching for him, she pulls him down into a kiss. What follows seems to convey a sense of orgasmic release – it is worth bearing in mind that Peckinpah was told to cut down this sequence by the film company even before it was submitted for a rating – and Charlie says, 'Sorry, Amy,' to which she responds, 'Hold me, hold me.' Immediately following this, we cut to David

Screen capture: Amy's response.

on the moor, finally successfully shooting down a bird. He runs eagerly to where it has fallen, but stops short as he sees it fluttering, dying in the bushes. The expression on his face is subtly delineated, but seems to imply pity and shame, emotions underlined as he cradles the dead bird in his hands. We cut once again to Charlie and Amy, embracing and kissing on the sofa, back to David returning the bird to lay it in the bushes; the camera zooms into close-up as he makes vain attempts to rub the blood from his hands off on his jersey.

The Second Rape

The scene cuts back to Charlie and Amy on the sofa, still making love. With a suddenness accentuated by a shift in tone and pace of the soundtrack, the camera offers a tight close-up of Charlie, one eye focused on something beyond the viewer. We cut to an extreme close-up of the business end of a double-barrelled shotgun; the camera tilts up to show Scutt's head and shoulders, and then back to Charlie's shocked expression, again in close-up.

There is another cut back to Scutt, who now has the shotgun raised and trained directly on Venner. Amy, facing away from the new arrival, is still unaware. Silent exchanges between Venner and Scutt follow, with Scutt motioning for Venner to move aside, Venner shaking his head, and Scutt taking two steps forward and raising the gun again, taking aim. Venner slowly moves and positions himself above Amy, who is now lying on her front on the sofa. She appears to smile as Charlie kisses the back of her neck and then moves away. An insert shot follows of Scutt unbuttoning his trousers. The next shot of Amy, a close-up, reveals Charlie's hand positioned just at the base of the back of her neck, and then we see Scutt closing in, kneeling down on the edge of the sofa. Now the flash cuts begin again as Amy realises something is wrong, struggles to look behind, then to get up off the couch, but Venner holds her down, his eyes fixed on Scutt. Amy finally manages to half-raise herself and we get a brief shot of what she sees: Scutt in medium close-up, moving in on her. The frames of Scutt are juxtaposed against a shot of Amy's wide-eyed, terrified face in close-up, the camera closing in as her mouth opens wide to scream, before her head is forced down again by Charlie. After a very brief cut back to David on the moor, his back to the camera, putting on his

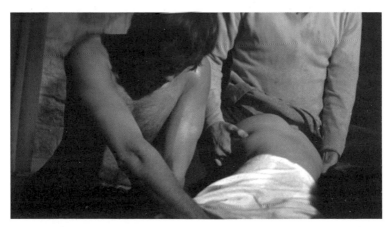

Screen capture: The second rape.

coat, we get the briefest of glimpses of Amy, Charlie and Scutt in a master shot, and it is clear that Charlie is crouched beside the sofa holding Amy down at the base of her neck, while Scutt enters her from behind. Presumably this is all that was left after the cuts demanded by the BBFC had been made (it is missing entirely from the shorter US edit). The original sequence infamously prompted a discussion between Melnick and Stephen Murphy of the BBFC over the precise nature of Scutt's attack – 'the exact direction of assault on Miss George', as Murphy delicately put it (bbfc Murphy, 1971b; see pp. 44–5). Equally infamously, the cuts Murphy suggested seem to have thrown the subject into a greater rather than a lesser state of ambiguity, but it is also the case that the rape is less protracted than it would otherwise have been.

Exactly what the original submitted cut did show will remain a mystery; the footage that hit the cutting-room floor is not extant. The US edit was even more severe, with the censor removing around thirty seconds of the sequence between Charlie and Amy, significantly reducing the sexual activity represented, and cutting around seventy seconds of the second rape in order to achieve the required 'R' rating. The sequence the US audiences saw had only a glimpse of Scutt unbuttoning his trousers, Amy screaming as she realises what is happening, and Charlie staring at Scutt, before the scene cut to David returning from the moor. What we are left with in the longer UK edit are shots of Amy, clearly in pain and distress, and Venner wincing at the brutality of the assault and, perhaps, at his own part in it. There is one more shot of David on the moor, a clearer view of Charlie holding Amy and Amy struggling, whimpering, and of Charlie raising his head to look at Scutt's grimacing face. Amy is half-choking under the pressure of the grip on her neck, but then we see a slight relaxation of the tension and agony, and a cut back to Scutt finds him moving away. Venner's face is hard to read – his disgust at Scutt perhaps confused by guilt at his own part in the action – and as Charlie stands up, still looking down at Amy, we see her, hair damp with sweat and matted across her face, as she presumably rolls over onto her back on the sofa and looks up at the two men. What might have been here

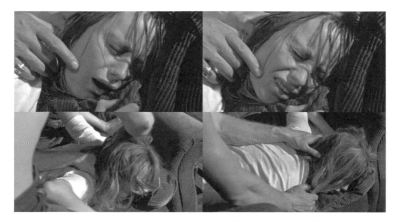

Screen captures: The second rape.

originally – dialogue between Amy and her two attackers (see p. 110) – is replaced by a cut back to David walking back towards the village at sunset.

Script Development of the Rape Scene

Tracing the development of the sequence through a number of draft scripts is a complex task, but reaps rewarding insights into the thinking behind this crucial sequence. As one might expect, it was one of the most heavily revised scenes in the screenplay after Peckinpah added it to the narrative in his first rewriting of Goodman's submission (SPC Goodman, 1970a, p. 46).[43] From the earliest drafts, Peckinpah emphasised Amy's sexual frustration, with directions such as 'She is worn out from struggling – worn out from need,' and, 'She tries to turn away then her body with a will of its own, rises to meet him .... Her own need matches his own' (SPC G&P, 1970b, pp. 83, 84, 84b). These early drafts depicted Charlie treating her roughly, followed by a more gentle lovemaking initiated by Amy. As the scene evolved through successive drafts, Venner also evolved, exchanging domineering brutalism for something more ambivalent. The editing of the scene was shaped similarly to emphasise, amongst other things, Venner's hatred of Scutt and his reluctance to hand Amy over to him; Peckinpah requested that a cut of Venner nodding to his workmate be dropped (SPC Peckinpah, 1971a, p. 5), although this may have been in response to one of Lew Rachmil's suggestions (SPC Rachmil, 1971d, p. 5).

Far more disturbingly, the first drafts of the script Peckinpah worked on were unequivocal about Amy's response to the second rape. As she is assaulted from behind by Scutt, the draft describes her as 'ready to scream – can't – makes the best of it – and the worst of it – wanton! She is insatiable and at first they react to her with delight' (SPC G&P, 1970b, p. 99). Goodman was unhappy with this version, protesting that 'I wouldn't turn her into a wanton at that point' (SPC Goodman, 1970b, p. 3). The same thinking presumably resulted in the excision of the earlier exchange between Charlie and Amy – 'You like it, don't you? … Yes … yes, Charlie … don't stop' – which was included in the 'as-shot' shooting script (SPC G&P, 1971c, p. 78). It may be that this was filmed and then cut as part of the concession to Rachmil's demands that the eroticism of the encounter should be toned down.

In a long memo with detailed notes on the screenplay, Melnick disputed this development of Amy's character: 'She isn't as much in need of getting laid as she is in need of feeling important – of having the power with someone,' he suggested. He referred also to Martin Baum's response to the draft, writing in the same memo to Peckinpah, 'Marty's big point here is that she shouldn't ultimately abandon herself to Scutt's rape. Probably after struggling and perhaps being subdued by Venner she would just lie there absolutely impassively.' He concludes, 'In any case there is no question but that we should feel terribly sorry for her both physically and psychically at the end of the scene.' Peckinpah's written annotation in response is a simple 'All OK' (SPC Melnick, 1970b, p. 11), and later drafts of the screenplay bear signs of appropriate changes: the 'makes the best of it – and the worst of it – wanton!' line quoted above is amended to: 'AMY TRIES TO SCREAM can't – tries to make the best of it can't – hating it – she looks up at Venner – hating him – he caresses her' (SPC G&P, 1971c, p. 80). The original draft also included some dialogue following the rape (the edit in the finished version of the film is abrupt – Amy's lips part as if to speak, but there is a sudden cut to a shot of David returning from the moors). This went through a number of different incarnations, but in general took one of three possible directions – in earlier versions, Amy mocked both Scutt and Venner (see, for example, SPC G&P, 1970c, p. 84c); in another, Charlie offered a callous quip as he left, 'Sorry you didn't enjoy it – we did' (SPC G&P, 1971a, p. 81); and in the third, Amy challenged Charlie over his betrayal (SPC G&P, 1971c, p. 78).

It is evident that there was a long and difficult journey from script to screen for this sequence – a much more convoluted one than for any other part of the film. The journey involved tough negotiations between director and star; disputes between director and production team over the script and then the editing; the joint efforts of Peckinpah and his team of editors; and further disputes over cuts with the BBFC and the MPAA. It is no surprise that it has since become the most hotly debated scene in the whole film.

Eroticising, Endorsing

If, as Prince,[44] Dukore, Fulwood (2002, p. 74), Weddle, Seydor, Simmons[45] and others claim, the rape scene does not endorse the rape myth, but instead offers us an insight into Amy's ravaged psyche, then there must have been quite a considerable overhaul of Peckinpah's original scripted plan for the scene; it is hard to read the drafts as anything other than crude male fantasy. Of course, what matters in the final analysis is not the process but the product: what questions does the finished film provoke? There can be no doubt that the final version is more complex and less overt in its endorsement of the male rape myth than it might have been if Peckinpah had not set to work to reshape the scene in the editing room in the way that he and his team did. Nevertheless, I find it hard to concur with Prince that, 'As the scene was revised and now exists, most of the sexual activity is implied, and the rape itself plays in medium shot and close-up' so that the focus is on Amy's 'emotional responses' and 'only secondarily' on the sexual acts (Prince, 1998, p. 137). While Prince is undoubtedly correct in his assessment of the emotional complexity of the scene (and Susan George's performance is extraordinary in her ability to convey it – Amy's failed marriage, her desperate sadness, a reawakened tenderness for her former lover Charlie), the rape scene itself is in parts brutal and in parts, I would argue, intended to be nothing but erotic.

Those who defend the film claim that the subjective camera angles, replicating Amy's point of view, place us inside the action, inside the violence, and make the audience experience the assault from her perspective. Prince refers to the correspondence between Peckinpah and the producers who complained that early edits of the scene were too explicit and too sexual, and makes the point that Peckinpah consequently decided to use more close-up shots, in flash-cutting mode, in order to impress upon the audience the experience of the rape as Amy feels it, such as in the confusing, upsetting overlay of images of Venner and David. I agree that, in this, he was largely successful. However, the scene is structured by an alternation between these rapid flash-cut sequences and longer periods dominated by medium-range

Screen capture: A typical master shot from the first rape.

master shots and lingering, medium close-up and close-up shots of Amy stripped half-naked. When Amy attempts to cover her breasts, Venner wrenches her arms away, presumably as much for the benefit of the majority of the audience as for himself. There is also a lingering moment over the snapping of Amy's knicker elastic, which conveys an erotic sense rather more strongly than it suggests a feeling of horror at what is being perpetrated.

According to Prince, as the scene plays out, Amy exhibits what he calls 'a measured response' to Charlie; though clearly still very upset at what is 'a terrible assault', Prince concedes, there is at the same time 'a tenderness in her response'. This seems to me to underplay the way in which the scene is moulded to eroticise the rape. The eroticism is certainly toned down a little in *visual* terms as the sequence proceeds, as Peckinpah drops the earlier, more graphic master shots, featuring largely unhindered views of Amy's naked body, in favour of more head-and-shoulder close-ups (though still with glimpses of Amy's breasts). But, even with less-revealing close-ups, the erotic charge of the scene is maintained by the evident change in Amy's very sexual response to Charlie; her protesting cries gradually modulate into sighs and moans of pleasure, and the same emotion registers in her face, and in her physical response to Venner, as her hands reach up to stroke his face, and she sighs and gasps, 'Easy.' My contention is that, while the rape that will follow conveys nothing but violation and humiliation, it is impossible not to read the encounter with Venner as, in the end, an erotically charged scene. Prince claims that it disturbs us because it is not giving us clear moral anchors, not telling us 'who is good and who is bad here'. But in fact what is at stake is something far more troubling – it is a precise representation of the rape myth that a woman can say 'no' but, when forced into intercourse in spite of her protests, may actually enjoy being abused.

However, the use of montage within the sequence undoubtedly complicates matters still further: while some of the intercut images are to be understood as suggesting Amy's state of mind – those shots lifted from their earlier lovemaking scene, match-cut to the images of Venner – others are undoubtedly authorial: the images of David on the moor. The classic montage technique, where intercut scenes are to be read in parallel, as mutual commentaries, is used to implicate David in the violence perpetrated against Amy. After all, he bullies Amy emotionally and belittles her in the first half of the film, and in the siege scene he will slap her and pull her by the hair, as Charlie does in the rape scene. The film suggests that David's pattern of behaviour – his failure to respond to challenges, his cowardice – are of a piece with his abuse of Amy, and she is as much a victim of her husband as she is of Venner and Scutt.[46]

As I have already noted, the US cut of the film features a much shorter rape scene, and Martin Barker argues that the discrepancy between the US and the UK versions of the film is significant; the UK version, he suggests, 'sexualised the scene in a particular way', but the American cut, he argues, *de-emphasises* the eroticism. This may be so. Certainly the US version reduced the length of the first rape, and removed the second rape almost entirely. However, there are a couple of important complications to point out here; first of all, Barker's claim (2006, pp. 7–8) that the US version is the 'standard' or 'preferred' version seems perverse: not only is the standard US and UK DVD edition now the 'uncut' (UK) version, Melnick considered the UK version the superior one – or at least that is what he assumed Peckinpah's position to be when he wired this message to him on 28 October 1971:

TRYING TO REACH YOU STOP ABC NEW YORK INSISTING ON RELEASING 'R' IN U.S. MARTY AND I DID WIN THE BATTLE AND GOT THEM TO AGREE TO RELEASE OUR VERSION IN LONDON STOP PLEASE CALL WHEN YOU CAN GET TO PHONE LOVE, MELNICK (SPC Melnick, 1971c)

However, the matter is even more complicated than this. Linda Ruth Williams points out in her essay for *Sight and Sound* that the juxtaposition of a first, eroticised rape against a second, brutal rape runs the risk of creating another dangerous myth. Amy's eventual receptive response to Venner suggests that there can be such a thing as a 'good' rape, as opposed to the 'bad', violent one that Scutt perpetrates. 'In the *Straw Dogs* discourse, rape is not necessarily negative', Williams concludes, 'it all depends on who's doing it to you' (Williams, 1995, p. 26). While one might argue that the binary is an unnecessary one – it is quite possible that both rapes are being represented as evil acts – it is, in the end, hard to deny that the two rapes (regardless of Peckinpah's intentions) provoke very different responses.

In the final analysis, the difficulty of an eroticised rape scene is going to remain intractable in a culture where sexual violence against women is, in political rhetoric, an abomination, but where, in real life, it remains endemic.[47] Of course, the way these matters should impact upon censorship and individual freedom is another matter entirely. The concluding section will consider a number of films made since *Straw Dogs* was first released that continue the controversies over the representation of rape, not by arguing over the rights and wrongs of Peckinpah's own creation, but by creating new interventions (deliberate or otherwise) into these difficult cross-currents of debate.

✖ PART 5

THE LEGACY OF *STRAW DOGS*

Straw Dogs, Survival Horror and Rape Revenge

Although much has been written about Peckinpah's influence on the cinema of violence, it is almost always *The Wild Bunch*, rather than *Straw Dogs*, which is the default reference text. There are a number of possible reasons for this: most obviously, *The Wild Bunch* came first, and so it tends to be seen as more ground-breaking in these terms; it is also unquestionably a milestone in the history of the Western, while *Straw Dogs* is harder to pigeon-hole in terms of genre. Third, the violence in *The Wild Bunch* is more pervasive, and the 'body count' considerably higher than in the later film. Finally, the controversy over the sexual violence in *Straw Dogs* complicates it considerably when we are attempting to assess the impact of the film on writers and directors who followed. A vague sense of taint lingers around *Straw Dogs*, something writer–director Rod Lurie sensed perhaps when, interviewed about his planned remake of the movie, he felt it necessary to remark of Amy's character, 'You can be certain that she's not going to be smiling in the rape in *my* film' (Douglas, 2007).[48]

One of the oddest aspects of the legacy of *Straw Dogs* is to do with its status as a progenitor of the so-called 'rape-revenge' genre, a surprisingly loose agglomeration that ranges from exploitative fare such as *I Spit on Your Grave* (1978; remake 2010) and *The Last House on the Left* (1972; remake 2009) to more 'respectable', mainstream films such as *The Accused* and *Eye for an Eye* (1996). Two French films which have been classified as rape-revenge stories caused the BBFC some concern early in the new millennium – *Irreversible* and *Baise-Moi* (the former left uncut, the latter censored for a fleeting 'hard-core' shot of penetration). The most striking irony of all this is that *Straw Dogs* is not a rape-revenge film at all: the violence of the siege scene has very little to do with Amy's rape; David knows nothing of what has happened to his wife;

and the man Amy shoots at the end of the film is Riddaway, not one of the men who raped her.

    Straw Dogs is cited less often for its impact on other genres, although it is sometimes mentioned, invariably in the same breath as *Deliverance* (1972), in discussions of so-called 'survival horror': films such as *The Texas Chainsaw Massacre* (1974; sequel 1986; remake 2003 and prequel 2006), *The Hills Have Eyes* (1977; part 2 1984; remake 2006 and sequel 2007), *Southern Comfort* (1981), *Wrong Turn* (2003; sequels 2007 and 2009), *Wolf Creek* (2004), the feminist-oriented *While She Was Out* (2008) and the British film *Eden Lake* (2008). The citizens-under-siege concept is another that *Straw Dogs* anticipates; notable forays include *Dead Calm* (1989), *Funny Games* (1997, Hollywood remake 2007), *Panic Room* (2002), *Trapped* (2002), *Cellular* (2004), *Hostage* (2005) and *The Strangers* (2008). Many of these films work with the premise that, arguably, Peckinpah himself had planned as central to *Straw Dogs*: the limits of liberal pacifism, and what ordinary people are capable of when hemmed in and forced to respond to extraordinary circumstances, as well as how audiences respond to such morally compromised figures: 'Someone may feel a strange, sick exultation at the violence,' Peckinpah told a *Rolling Stone* journalist, 'But he should ask himself, "What is going on in my heart?"' (SPC Hodenfield, 1971, p. 12). On the other hand, very few of those mentioned above seem concerned with much beyond the visceral thrills of the tension created by sustained threat, and the release of explosive violence.

    However, it is not in the survival horror or the rape-revenge genre that the most visible traces of the legacy of *Straw Dogs* inhere. The unfortunate if inevitable truth remains that it is in the censorship and certification conundrums circulating around the depiction of sexual violence that *Straw Dogs* has had its most enduring influence. This first became evident when Peckinpah's film was under review at the BBFC at the same time that an uncut *The Last House on the Left* had also been resubmitted for home-video certification (see pp. 64–6). Both *Last House* and Meir Zarchi's *I Spit on Your Grave* date from the 1970s, although it was in the 1980s that their profiles were raised amongst cult-cinema buffs: both were included on the Director of

Public Prosecution's list of films likely to be found obscene by the UK courts. (*The Last House on the Left* had failed to secure a cinema certification in the UK when submitted in 1974). *Last House* may be more artful than *I Spit* (it claims to draw inspiration from Ingmar Bergman's 1960 film *The Virgin Spring*), but both are disturbing, rough-and-ready pieces of film-making that offer up spectacles of objectification and abjection of the female body. Furthermore, they have also both been subjected to the remake/remodel treatment in the new millennium, and the deliberations of various censorship and certification bodies over the remakes are also illuminating.

In *The Last House on the Left*, members of a gang humiliate, rape and murder two young women. They later find themselves, inadvertently, in the family home of one of their victims, and when the parents discover the crime, they enact their revenge with an assortment of improvised weaponry. The film has been championed by high-profile film critic Mark Kermode in the UK, who accused the BBFC of inconsistency in its censorship, suggesting that its judgements were influenced by a paternalistic slant which allowed art-house films to get away with far more than mainstream fare (though whether *Last House* could be described as mainstream is a moot point; see Egan, 2007, pp. 229–32 for further discussion of Kermode's campaign). As discussed in the earlier analysis of the certification of an uncut *Straw Dogs* in the UK for home video (see pp. 55–67), the fortunes of *Last House* and *Straw Dogs* were tangled and knotted together by this point. The BBFC finally passed *Last House* uncut in March 2008; up until then, the most complete UK release was cut by thirty-one seconds. The film's detailed depiction of extreme, sadistic violence perpetrated on random victims anticipates, in some ways, the torture-porn vogue of the second half of the 2000s. In an era of film-making where such spectacles are now commonplace, it could be argued that continued efforts to censor *Last House* would have constituted, if you will pardon the phrase, sheer bloody-mindedness. The Board's decision to grant it a certificate in its unedited form is a cause for celebration amongst those preoccupied with the hallowed 'uncut' status of such movies, or, more generally, with the principle that adults should be permitted to decide for themselves what they wish to view. Whether the world is a better place with an uncut *Last House on the Left* in it is another matter.

I Spit on Your Grave, however, is clearly still regarded in a different light by the BBFC. Meir Zarchi's rape-revenge tale is a cheap and nasty piece of work, with acting and production values even poorer than those on offer in *Last House*. It features multiple acts of rape visited upon the same victim filmed in a graphic, but flat (some might say inept) style. Jennifer (Camille Keaton), a city type sojourning in the country in order to find peace to write her novel, is set upon by a gang of local rednecks. Having shown, seemingly interminably, the terrible things that befall Jennifer (rape, beating, sodomy, having a bottle inserted in her vagina), the film proceeds to detail her acts of revenge, which include the masturbation/castration of one of her attackers in a shared foam bath, a hanging and death by outboard engine. The fact that this movie has received far more attention than it ever deserved is due in large part to the way in which cult movies build their audiences and reputations, but film scholars and critics have also played a role, particularly as part of the liberal impetus to counter over-eager right-wing censoriousness. In the collection of essays rushed out at the time of the 'video-nasty' scare in the UK, Martin Barker's *The Video Nasties: Freedom and Censorship in the Media* (1984), Marco Starr attempted to mount a defence of the film, claiming it powerfully transmitted the horror of the act of rape; and Carol Clover devoted considerable space to it in *Men, Women and Chainsaws* (1992), seeing it as a pretension-stripped incarnation of *The Accused:* 'the story of a gang-raped woman hell-bent on revenge' (p. 151). The director, in a commentary track for a special-edition DVD, laughably claims the film as a feminist piece, and fans of the film have parroted his, and others', apologia endlessly (see Egan, 2007, pp. 146–7). Such delusions are summarily dispatched by Barbara Creed, who demonstrates the work's irredeemable misogyny (1993, pp. 128–31), pointing out how Jennifer is 'symbolically and literally transformed into a battered, bleeding wound' (p. 131).

The film remains unavailable uncut in the UK (the BBFC originally demanded over seven minutes of edits), and a more recent reissue, trumpeting a restored version, has simply reframed the sequences the BBFC rejected, or else inserted repeated shots in clumsy edits.[49] The Board remains adamant that the film in its uncut form features 'shots of nudity that tend to eroticise sexual violence and shots of humiliation that tend to endorse sexual violence by encouraging viewer complicity in sexual humiliation and rape' (BBFC, 2010). When yet another home-video reissue was submitted in 2010 (an 'Ultimate Collector's Edition' from 101 Films), almost three minutes of cuts were demanded. The Irish Film Classification Office was even harsher, rejecting it entirely on account of its depiction of 'acts of gross violence and cruelty towards humans' (Clarke, 2010).

Remake/Remodel

Directed by Dennis Iliadis, *The Last House on the Left* remake was released in 2009, and rated '18' by the BBFC. However, the extended classification information about the film usefully clarifies by example the principles and the distinctions that now define the Board's practice when examiners are dealing with scenes of sexual violence. The report noted that the rape scene 'went beyond the "discreet and brief" depiction of sexual assault that is allowed by the BBFC Guidelines at "15"'. It continues:

> However, the focus on the girl's anguish and the lack of sexualised nudity or graphic sexual detail means that the scene did not 'eroticise or endorse sexual assault' and therefore did not require intervention beyond the '18' category. (BBFC, 2009b)

Certainly the remake eschews the pornographic potential of the original, which featured the two young female victims being forced to have sex with one another for the voyeuristic pleasure of their tormentors. As the BBFC's description notes, the rape is shot with minimal nudity, and the film manages to evoke a sense of unease and tension in the scenes leading up to the encounter with Krug's (Garret Dillahunt) gang. The emphasis falls much more heavily than it does in the original on the build-up to the parents' discovery of the identity of the gang, and the brutal retribution they enact. In this sense, the film exchanges the nihilism of torture porn for a more straightforward invitation to the audience to engage with and, indeed, relish the acts of revenge. In the US, the film had been cut to achieve an 'R', and the company released 'theatrical' ('R'-rated) and 'Unrated' versions on DVD and Blu-Ray, as has become common with films featuring extensive and graphic violence.

The remake of *I Spit on Your Grave*, however, proved more difficult for the certification bodies on both sides of the Atlantic. In the US, the company took the unusual step of setting up a limited theatrical release for the *I Spit on Your Grave* remake in its uncut, unrated form, after the MPAA refused to grant it an 'R' rating. In the UK, it was cut by forty-three seconds for a potential UK theatrical release. The extended details explain:

> Company was required to make a total of seventeen cuts during three separate scenes of sexual violence in order to remove potentially harmful material (in this case, shots of nudity that tend to eroticise sexual violence and shots of humiliation that tend to endorse sexual violence by encouraging viewer complicity in sexual humiliation and rape). Cuts made in accordance with BBFC Guidelines and policy. (BBFC, 2010)

The report goes on to single out other elements subject to cuts that the Board felt tended to endorse the act (for example, 'by encouraging viewer complicity by the use of camcorder footage, filmed by the rapists') or eroticise it ('through the use of nudity'). The Extended Classification Information concludes that,

> With these cuts made, the film's scenes of *very strong terrorisation and sexual violence* remain potentially shocking, distressing or offensive to some adult viewers, but are also likely to be found repugnant and to be aversive. They are not credibly likely to encourage imitation. [emphasis in the original] (BBFC, 2010)

The information notes that the nudity during the rape scene is only 'incidental' in the cut version, and that 'the most likely response to the cut version of the scenes is revulsion and disgust rather than excitement or arousal' (BBFC, 2010).

Once more, the key factors are those that informed the debates around *Straw Dogs,* and not only at the Board; as my analysis has shown, the concerns about *eroticising* and *endorsing* underpinned the agonising over the rape scene in the film from the earliest stages of script development. Almost thirty years later, for the BBFC to justify, finally, the uncut release of *Straw Dogs,* the Board had to deploy the depiction of the second, violent rape as a crucial element in its rationale. Because the rape perpetrated by Scutt is so brutal and upsetting, it was decided, after all, that the film as a whole did *not* endorse the 'rape myth', even though the BBFC had maintained as late as 1999, in press statements, annual reports and interviews, that it did precisely that (see pp. 59–60). Furthermore, the first rape was now viewed as one 'filmed in a relatively discreet manner, with limited potential today for titillation' (BBFC, 2002a).

The reversal is more than a little perplexing: as the close analysis indicates, the sex scene between Charlie and Amy, though presumably trimmed from earlier, more explicit rough cuts in response to Rachmil's insistent notes (see pp. 18–19), remains a problem in terms of 'eroticising', no matter how cast, crew, critics or Board examiners might wish to play down the extent of the nudity. If the BBFC wishes to argue that the scene has 'limited potential *today* for titillation' [my emphasis], one is tempted to ask, in what sense is the scene less erotic now than it might have been thirty years earlier? And how does one square the objection to camcorder footage in the *Spit* remake with the shots in *Straw Dogs* that put the audience in line with Venner's point of view? Once again, the arguments come full circle: the BBFC's deliberations and, effectively, the incorporation of their own stage of editing into the process of shaping the final version of the film that will be shown in cinemas, relate directly to the kind of interventions that Farber and Changas exposed in the procedures adopted by the MPAA in the late 60s and early 70s (see pp. 31–4). The Board's concluding remarks about the cuts to the *Spit* remake, noted above, are freighted with an unspoken assumption that the film is a 'better' one because the rape is no longer either eroticising or endorsing the sexual violence.[50]

Straw Dogs, then, can be seen as a key progenitor for a set of films that put themselves on a collision course with censors preoccupied with sexual violence. When a new film such as the *Spit* remake appears, the questions over titillation (eroticising), and the idea of 'endorsing' the act of rape, recur, and it becomes increasingly difficult to fashion anything that could be considered an objective form of measurement.

Closing Thoughts

Straw Dogs has been one of the most troubling and troublesome films the BBFC has had to deal with in terms of the cinematic representation of sexual violence. As we can see from recent cases, the rape scene in Peckinpah's film has become a kind of guilty subconscious for the BBFC, hovering at its shoulder whenever it is confronted with another movie addressing the issue of rape via direct representation of the crime itself. Even ten years after its release uncut on home video, the ramifications of the BBFC's agonised hand-wringing over it are still evident. Looking back over these films that exist in the shadow of Peckinpah's movie, the significance of the debate over the second rape in *Straw Dogs* is startling. Dan Melnick recalls having to sit with Stephen Murphy analysing the footage frame by frame, convincing him that what he was seeing was not anal intercourse but rear entry. What Peckinpah had fought over – with his screenwriter, with his female lead, with his producer and the ratings-nervous team at ABC Pictures, and then (via Melnick) with the censors – came down to this: effectively, a bizarre clash between generational and national cultures. The distinction Melnick and Murphy deliberated over was a vital one at the time; today, it seems oddly quaint and of little significance in terms of censorship decisions (*Irreversible,*

The Accused, *I Spit on Your Grave* and the *Last House* remake, for example, imply or depict anal rape).

Nevertheless, the distinction *is* significant, and can be interpreted as another index of BBFC policy. It is clear that the Board is pursuing a specific agenda in terms of gender politics: the sexual assaults it finds acceptable are those that are constructed as unerotic; demarcated as acts of power and domination rather than sexual gratification. The fact that this is in line with much psychological, criminological and sociological research about rape is presumably not coincidental: since the late 1970s, feminist-inflected approaches have shifted the emphasis on rape to interpret it as an act of violence rather than sex.[51] Ironically enough, thirty years on, the BBFC's ongoing efforts to reshape scenes of sexual violence in line with its stance against eroticising and endorsing mean that the sequence that troubled Stephen Murphy (and the critics) the most in 1971 becomes the least problematic for a contemporary examiner, because it is less likely to endorse or eroticise the act of rape. On the other hand, as Martin Barker has noted, there is always a 'high degree of variability in strategies of reading film, and the conclusions reached by different viewers' (Barker, 2005, p. 35). Finally, such intractable issues of directorial intention and predictions of (and/or judgements upon) audience response leave the door open to challenges that the BBFC's arbitrations remain ... frustratingly arbitrary.[52]

In the final analysis, if *Straw Dogs* does still have the power to disturb us, its power resides in the way in which Peckinpah is able to provoke, simultaneously, such conflicting responses. In a time witnessing a continuing revolution in attitudes towards gender and sexuality, *Straw Dogs* remains volatile; whether this has more to do with its grim determination to cling to outmoded gender politics than it does with the film's undeniable artistry is a moot point. Peckinpah's film remains, perhaps in spite of itself, a valuable catalyst for reigniting crucial debates.

✖ APPENDICES

Appendix A: Key Details

Cast

David Sumner	Dustin Hoffman	Bertie Hedden	Michael Mundell*
Amy Sumner	Susan George	John Niles	Peter Arne
Tom Hedden	Peter Vaughan	Harry Ware	Robert Keegan
Major Scott	T. P. McKenna	Mrs Hedden	June Brown**
Charlie Venner	Del Henney	Emma Hedden	Chloe Frank**
Norman Scutt	Ken Hutchison	Louise Hood	Cherina Mann
Reverend Barney Hood	Colin Welland	Henry Niles	David Warner*
Chris Cawsey	Jim Norton		
Janice Hedden	Sally Thomsett	(*uncredited in the film's title and	
Riddaway	Donald Webster	credit sequences)	
Bobby Hedden	Len Jones	(** scenes deleted)	

Production Crew

Director	Sam Peckinpah	Camera Operator	Herbert Smith
Producer	Daniel Melnick	Editors	Paul Davies,
Screenplay	Sam Peckinpah and		Roger
	David Z. Goodman		Spottiswoode and
Music	Jerry Fielding		Tony Lawson
Orchestrator	Lennie Niehaus*		Bob Wolfe
Associate Producer	James Swann	Sound Editor	Garth Craven
Production Supervisor	Derek Kavanagh	Sound Recordist	John Bramall
Production Assistant	George Davis*	Sound Dialogue Editor	Michael Ellis*
Director of Photography	John Coquillon, BSC	Special Effects	John Richardson

Casting	Miriam Brickman	Make-up Assistant	Peter Frampton*
Design Consultant	Julia Trevelyan Oman	Chief Hairdresser	Bobbie Smith
Production Designer	Ray Simm	Continuity	Pamela Davies
Art Director	Ken Bridgeman	First Assistant Director	Terry Marcel
Set Dresser	Peter James	Wardrobe Supervisor	Tiny Nicholls
Stunt Coordinator	Bill Cornelius	Stills Photographer	John Jay*
Stunts	Peter Brayham* and	Unit Publicist	Brian Doyle*
	Joe Dunne*	Dialogue Director	Katy Haber
Stunt Double: S. George	Sue Longhurst*	Title Designer	Anthony Goldschmidt
Body Double: S. George	Susan Shaw*	Assistant Director	Terry Marcel
Make-up Supervisor	Harry Frampton		(*uncredited)

ABC Pictures

President	Martin Baum	Production Supervisor	Lewis J. Rachmil

Other Details

Locations
Exteriors in Cornwall, England: St Buryan, Penzance (Wakely); Lamorna Cove, Lamorna;
Tor Noon, Morvah (Trencher's Farm).
Interiors: Twickenham Film Studios, Middlesex, England

Awards
Nominated for Best Music, Original Dramatic Score (Jerry Fielding), Academy Awards,
1972.
Won Best Director at the Kansas City Film Critics Circle Awards, 1972.

Shooting details
Footage shot: 261,195 feet.
Production began 22 January 1971; shooting suspended for five days mid-February due to
Peckinpah's illness; final day of photography: 29 April 1971.
Total negative cost: $3,251,794.

Release dates
25 November 1971 (UK); 29 December 1971 (USA)

Censorship and certification worldwide
Argentina: '18'
Australia: 'R' (original rating); MA (DVD re-rating, 2004)
Brazil: '18'
Canada: 13+
Finland: 'K-18' cut, 1971; 'K-18' uncut, 1981
France: '16'
Germany: '18' (original rating); '16' (re-rating, 2007)
Hong Kong: 'III' (i.e. 18+)
Iceland: '16'
Ireland: '18'
Italy: 'VM18' (original rating); VM14 (re-rating)
Japan: 'R-15'
New Zealand: 'R18'
Norway: '18'
South Korea: '18'
Spain: '18'
Sweden: '15'
UK: original release 'X'; banned (1987); re-certification '18' (2002)
US: 'R' (cut); released uncut as unrated version on home video (1996)[53]

Appendix B: Notes

1 This anecdotal impression is endorsed by Martin Barker's research into audience responses to the film (see Barker, 2005).

2 Both films were remade in recent years, the former in 2010 and the latter in 2009. The originals and their remakes are discussed in Part 5.

3 According to editor Roger Spottiswoode, Peckinpah got his own back by scripting the scene depicting David's awkward encounter with the vicar Barney Hood and his wife as a parody of Pinter's style (Novak, 2002).

4 Sally Thomsett is actually three months older than Susan George, even though her character was clearly intended to be several years younger than Amy.

5 Warner's version of events can be heard in an interview included on the German DVD release, *Straw Dogs / Wer Gewalt sät …*, EuroVideo, 2007.

6 Hutchison tells the amusing anecdote at some length in the Channel 4 documentary *Man Trap* (2003). The 'dog brother' moniker comes from a memo Peckinpah sent him in March 1971 (SPC Peckinpah, 1971c).

7 Katy Haber commentary track, Fremantle UK DVD release, 2002.

8 The term 'stop' was conventionally used in dictating telegram messages to indicate the end of a sentence.

9 'I Was Peckinpah's Girl Friday', broadcast 4 November 2007, 13:30 on BBC Radio 4.

10 Dan Melnick interview, Criterion US DVD release, 2003. However, according to McKenna himself, it was another man who had been dancing on the table with a prostitute, and both fell on top of him and fractured his shoulder when the table gave way beneath them (Kermode, 2003, p. 9).

11 Fremantle DVD, 2002.

12 Fremantle DVD commentary track, 2002.

13 In the commentary on the Fremantle release, Haber seems a little mystified as the screening continues and it becomes evident from the camera angles in the final cut that George was not replaced at any point. Haber concludes that none of the body-double footage was used in the final cut, although it is possible that the very fleeting shot that remains of the anal/rear-entry rape in medium shot is body-double footage (see p. 107).

14 This phrase would recur in later discourse about the film: see pp. 12–13.

15 Fremantle DVD, 2002.

16 See also other interviews and features from this period, e.g. Thomson, 2002 (apparently quoting Peckinpah), Campion, 2002 and (quoting Susan George) Das, 2003.

17 Interview on Fremantle DVD, 2002.

18 In a 2003 interview, asked if she herself felt violated by the scene, George replied, 'Well, that is your choice of words but obviously Amy was violated and I was playing Amy so therefore Susan George was violated too' (Das, 2003, p. 25).

19 Whether this is an accurate assessment will be discussed in Part 4.

20 One report that the bin was set alight gave rise to the popular characterisation of feminist demonstration as 'bra-burning'.

21 In the edition of *Variety* that carried a review of *Straw Dogs* (1 December 1971), the first page ran a story noting that, 'The number of locations in the midtown area devoted to the showing of hardcore porno pix is fast outstripping the conventional theatrical sites.'

22 Farber repeated his criticism of the MPAA's decision in his review for *Cinema* magazine, noting that, 'The second rape has been shortened and the horror of the experience muted' (Farber, 1972b, p. 5).

23 Presumably to Murphy's chagrin, Palmer, Coleman and Alexander Walker all made a point of identifying Scutt's attack as anal rape.

24 It is worth noting that one of the signatories, the *Guardian* writer Derek Malcolm, had written in his own review that, while he expected it to be attacked 'for gratuitous sexual and other violence', he did not himself think there was 'anything gratuitous about it at all' (Malcolm, 1971). Others who signed included Cashin, Coleman, Hinxman, Melly, Walker and Powell.

25 Extant production stills, including one with a camera fixed to the bonnet and Hoffman and McKenna seated in the car, suggest the scene may have been filmed.

26 For full discussion, see Petley (2011); Barker and Petley (2001); Martin (2007); Fgan (2007).

27 I would like to acknowledge my debt to Craig Lapper's work on the timeline of submissions of the film for home-video certification in the pages that follow. His essay is included as a DVD extra on the Fremantle DVD.

28 When *Straw Dogs* was included in a season of Peckinpah movies at the National Film Theatre, London, in January 2009, it appears that this was the print used for the screenings, despite the fact that by then the uncut version had been in circulation on home video for over six years.

29 This problem had been identified by two former MPAA interns, Stephen Farber and Estelle Changas, back in 1971. See p. 33.

30 Letters quoted from the James Ferman Collection, Box 49 ('Original Notes File'), held at the BFI Library, London.

31 A curious case of *déjà vu* recalling a previous right-wing backlash rejection when Nixon dismissed the findings of his Commission on Obscenity and Pornography, twenty years earlier (see p. 27).

32 See Barker, 2005, for further discussion.

33 Thanks to Peter Woods for detailed information in this respect.

34 I am grateful to Peter Woods for additional information on the BBFC's deliberations over the certification of the film for home-video release.

35 Typically, contemporary reviews seemed more concerned with the siege scene than the sexual violence; William Johnson's 1972 review for *Film Quarterly* noted that 'Controversy has raged over the violence of this climactic sequence' and mentioned the rape scene only in passing (Johnson, 1972, p. 62).

36 The painting, by Lorraine Schneider, became a popular poster amongst the protesters against the Vietnam conflict, and was adopted as its symbol by the organisation Another Mother for Peace (AMP).

37 In a 2003 interview, Hoffman remarked that, 'I was against the war in Vietnam and yet violence also attracted me, and I thought that maybe I could put some of that into the character' (Kermode, 2003, p. 9).

38 An earlier draft was more explicit: 'No this is my house – this is where I live – it's your country – but [gesturing] this is mine…' [SPC G&P, 1970c, Peckinpah pencil notes on reverse of p. 107].

39 Earlier drafts of the script also included more elaborate traps such as a window frame wired to electrocute anyone who touches it (SPC G&P, 1970i, unpaginated script note).

40 Hoffman uses the term in an interview for the *Mantrap* documentary; he felt that they did not develop the idea in the representation of their relationship as much as they might have done.

41 Unless noted otherwise, the references to Prince in this section derive from his commentary track on the Criterion DVD, 2003.

42 This line caused some confusion and debate in the editing process: Lew Rachmil suggested that it required attention 'in looping or a substitution as I do not think an American audience will ever understand the word "reave"' (SPC Rachmil, 1971d). However, the line remained intact, and its dialect, archaic quality is in keeping with Venner's character.

43 Goodman's original screenplay had included a confrontation at the farmhouse between Louise/Amy and Venner, but it ends after he attempts a coarse seduction, and Louise picks up the phone to call the police.

44 Criterion DVD commentary track, 2003.

45 Fremantle DVD commentary track, 2002.

46 I am indebted to Brian Woolland for discussion of this point.

47 In 2004, it was reported that, in the US alone, a woman is raped every ninety seconds (Amnesty International, 2004).

48 Three and a half years later, the remake is finally complete, but it has been the victim of repeated rescheduling, and is finally due out some time in 2011.

49 For anyone who wishes to subject themselves to it, it is available uncut on the US unrated DVD 'millennium edition'.

50 The BBFC still retains its power to surprise us. In its 2007 annual report, it was noted that the 1970s soft-porn movie *Emmanuelle* was finally being passed uncut. The film had always had various edits required in previous submissions, notably to the rape scene, for alleged eroticised violence. In 2007, however, 'it was judged that in the full context of an uncut classification it was clearer that there was no endorsement of the "rape myth"': once again, the decision to allow more frames to remain intact actually resulted in a more 'satisfactory' film, by the standards of the BBFC and its guidelines. On the other hand, the 1968 film *Venus in Furs* was still subject to cuts in its rape scene because 'it was felt to endorse "rape myth" attitudes' (BBFC, 2007, p. 74).

51 See, for example, Brownmiller (1975); Gavey (2004); for a re-evaluation of this position, see Bourke (2007).

52 For a detailed discussion of the BBFC and sexual violence, see Chapter 13 of Julian Petley's *Film and Video Censorship in Contemporary Britain* (2011).

53 Information adapted from http://www.imdb.com/title/tt0067800/ [accessed 26 June 2009].

Appendix C: References

Section 1: Books, Essays, Articles, Reviews

Aldgate, Anthony and Robertson, James C. (2005) *Censorship in Theatre and Cinema*, Edinburgh: Edinburgh University Press.

Amnesty International (2004) 'Amnesty International Launches Global Campaign to Stop Violence against Women – a "Cancer" and "Human Rights Atrocity". Available from: http://www.amnesty.org.uk/news_details.asp?NewsID=15231 [accessed 21 September 2010].

Anon (1970) *The Obscenity Report*, Introduction by John Trevelyan, London: Olympia Press.

Anon, imdb (2002) 'News for *Straw Dogs*'. Available from: http://www.imdb.com/title/tt0067800/news?year=2002 [accessed 16 February 2011].

Ardrey, Robert (1961) *African Genesis: A Personal Investigation into the Animal Origins and Nature of Man*, New York: Dell.

Barker, Martin (ed.) (1984) *The Video Nasties: Freedom and Censorship in the Media*, London: Pluto Press.

Barker, Martin (2005) 'Loving and Hating *Straw Dogs:* The Meanings of Audience Responses to a Controversial Film', Particip@tions vol. 2 no. 2. Available from: http://www.participations.org/volume%202/issue%202/2_02_barker.htm [accessed 16 October 2006].

Barker, Martin (2006) 'Loving and Hating *Straw Dogs:* The Meanings of Audience Responses to a Controversial Film' Part 2: Rethinking *Straw Dogs* as a Film', Particip@tions vol. 3 no.1. Available from: http://www.participations.org/volume%203/issue%201/3_01_barker.htm [accessed 16 October 2006].

Barker, Martin and Julian Petley (eds) (2001) *Ill Effects: the Media-Violence Debate*, 2nd edn, London: Routledge.

Barr, Charles (1972) '*Straw Dogs, A Clockwork Orange* and the Critics', *Screen* vol. 13 no. 2 (Summer), pp. 17–31.

BBFC (undated) 'Case Studies: *Straw Dogs*'. Available from: http://www.sbbfc.co.uk/ CaseStudies/Straw_Dogs [accessed 21 September 2010].

BBFC (1999) Annual Report 1999. Available from: http://www.bbfc.co.uk/downloads/pub/ BBFC%20Annual%20Reports/BBFC_AnnualReport_1999.pdf [accessed 2 July 2008].

BBFC (2002a) Press release: 'BBFC Passes Straw Dogs on Cut on Video'. Available from: http://www.bbfc.co.uk/news/press/20020701.html [accessed 17 July 2008].

BBFC (2002b) Annual Report 2002. Available from: http://www.bbfc.co.uk/downloads/pub/ BBFC%20Annual%20Reports/BBFC_AnnualReport_2002.pdf [accessed 17 July 2008].

BBFC (2002c) *The Last House on the Left* classification record, BBFC reference BVF060117, Extended Classification Information. Available from: http://www.bbfc.co.uk/ website/Classified.nsf/0/ae4f890aeaf8fec680256bfb0031d829?OpenDocument& ExpandSection=2#_Section2 [accessed 26 June 2009].

BBFC (2007) Annual Report 2007. Available from: http://www.bbfc.co.uk/download/ annual-reports/BBFC AnnualReport_2007.pdf [accessed 6 December 2010].

BBFC (2009a) *Classification Guidelines*. Available from: http://www.bbfc.co.uk/download/ guidelines/BBFC%20Classification%20Guidelines%202009.pdf [accessed 2 December 2010].

BBFC (2009b) *The Last House on the Left* classification record, BBFC reference AFF256738, Extended Classification Information. Available from: http://www.bbfc.org/ website/Classified.nsf/c2fb077ba3f9b33980256b4f002da32c/8022031e484af4878025757 5005ebe30?OpenDocument&ExpandSection=1#_Section1 [accessed 26 June 2009].

BBFC (2010) *I Spit on Your Grave* classification record, BBFC reference BFF271143, Extended Classification Information. Available from: http://www.bbfc.org/BFF271143 [accessed 23 September 2010].

Bilton, Michael and Kevin Sim (1992) *Four Hours in My Lai: A War Crime and Its Aftermath*, New York: Penguin.

Bourke, Joanna (2007) *Rape: A History from 1960 to the Present Day*, London: Virago.

Brownmiller, Susan (1975) *Against Our Will: Men, Women and Rape*, New York: Simon & Schuster.

Bryson, John (1974) 'The Wild Bunch in New York', *New York Magazine,* 19 August, pp. 25–8; reprinted in Kevin J. Hayes (ed.) (2008) *Sam Peckinpah Interviews,* Jackson: University Press of Mississippi, pp. 137–44.

Campion, Chris (2002) *Daily Telegraph*, 28 September, p. 13.

Clarke, Donald (2010) 'Re-release of "I Spit on Your Grave" Banned by Film Body', *Irish Times*, 21 September. Available from: http://www.irishtimes.com/newspaper/ireland/2010/0921/1224279369319.html [accessed 24 September 2010].

Clover, Carol (1992) *Men, Women and Chainsaws*, London: BFI.

Coleman, John (1971) Review, *New Statesman*, 26 November.

Cook, David A. (2000) *Lost Illusions: American Cinema in the Shadow of Watergate and Vietnam 1970–1979*, Berkeley: University of California Press.

Cooke, David and Julian Petley (2007) 'In Conversation', in Philip French and Julian Petley (eds) *Censoring the Moving Image*, Oxford, New York and Calcutta: Seagull Books.

Creed, Barbara (1993) *The Monstrous Feminine: Film, Feminism, Psychoanalysis*, London and New York: Routledge.

Cumberbatch, Guy (2002) *Where Do You Draw the Line? Attitudes and Reactions of Video Renters to Sexual Violence in Film*, London: Communications Research Group.

Das, Linda (2003) *Evening Standard*, 7 August, p. 25.

Davy, Charles (ed.) (1938) *Footnotes to the Film*, London: Lovat Dickson.

Doggett, Peter (2007) *There's a Riot Going On: Revolutionaries, Rock Stars, and the Rise and Fall of '60s Counter-Culture*, Edinburgh: Canongate.

Donnelly, Mark (2005) *Sixties Britain: Culture, Society and Politics*, London: Longman.

Douglas, Edward (2007) 'EXCL: Rod Lurie on the *Straw Dogs* Remake', www.comingsoon. net. Available from: http://www.comingsoon.net/news/movienews.php?id=36434 [accessed 6 December 2010].

Dukore, Bernard F. (1999) *Sam Peckinpah's Feature Films*, Urbana: University of Illinois Press.

Echols, Alice (1994) '"Nothing Distant about It:" Women's Liberation and Sixties Radicalism,' in David Farber (ed.) *The Sixties: From Memory to History*, Chapel Hill: University of North Carolina Press, pp. 149–74.

Egan, Kate (2007) *Trash or Treasure? Censorship and the Changing Meaning of the Video Nasties*, Manchester and New York: Manchester University Press.

Ehrenreich, Barbara, Elizabeth Hess and Gloria Jacobs (1986) *Re-making Love: The Feminization of Sex*, Garden City, NY: Anchor.

Farber, Stephen (1972a) *The Movie Rating Game*, Washington, DC: Public Affairs Press.

Farber, Stephen (1972b) '*Straw Dogs*', *Cinema* vol. 7 no. 2, Issue no. 3 (Spring), pp. 2–7.

Farber, Stephen (2009) Email to the author, 27 March.

Fine, Marshall (2005) *Bloody Sam: The Life and Films of Sam Peckinpah*, New York: Hyperion.

Fulwood, Neil (2002) *The Films of Sam Peckinpah*, London: B. T. Batsford.

Gavey, Nicola (2004) *Just Sex? The Cultural Scaffolding of Rape*, London: Routledge.

Gitlin, Todd (1993) *The Sixties: Years of Hope, Days of Rage*, New York: Bantam Books.

Haber, Katy (2009) Email to the author, 8 April.

Haskell, Molly (1974) *From Reverence to Rape: The Treatment of Women in the Movies*, 2nd edn, 1987, Chicago, IL: University of Chicago Press.

Hoberman, J. (2003) *The Dream Life: Movies, Media and the Mythology of the Sixties*, New York: New Press.

Hodgkiss, Ros (undated) 'Arbitrary Decisions, an Autocratic Regime and No Accountability …'. Available from: http://www.melonfarmers.co.uk/arbbfcco.htm [accessed 2 July 2008].

Johnson, William (1972) '*Straw Dogs*', *Film Quarterly* vol. 26 no. 1 (Fall), pp. 61–4.

Kael, Pauline (1972) '*Straw Dogs*', *New Yorker* no. 47, 29 January, pp. 80–5.

Kermode, Mark (2001) 'Left on the Shelf', *Sight and Sound*, July. Available from: http://www.bfi.org.uk/sightandsound/feature/404 [accessed 26 June 2009].

Kermode, Mark (2003) *Observer*, review section, 3 August, pp. 9–10.

Lapper, Craig (2001) Email to Peter Woods, 23 July.

Levy, Ariel (2005) *Female Chauvinist Pigs: Women and the Rise of Raunch Culture*, London: Pocket Books.

Lewis, Jon (2000) *Hollywood v. Hard Core: How the Struggle over Censorship Saved the Modern Film Industry*, New York and London: New York University Press.

Malcolm, Derek (1971) *Straw Dogs* review, *Guardian*, 25 November.

Maltby, Richard (2003) *Hollywood Cinema*, 2nd edn, Oxford: Blackwell.

Martin, John (2007) *Seduction of the Gullible: The Truth behind the Video Nasty Scandal*, London: Stray Cat Publishing.

Mediawatch (2003) 'Violence in the Media – Survey of Films 2003', *Mediwatchuk.org.uk*. Available from: http://www.mediawatchuk.org.uk/index2.php?option=com_content&do_pdf=1&id=315 [accessed 12 July 2008].

Melonfarmers (2003) UK News, Autumn. Available from: http://www.melonfarmers.co.uk/arne03d.htm [accessed 14 July 2008].

Morgan, Robin (1974) 'Theory and Practice: Pornography and Rape', in L. J. Lederer (ed.) (1980) *Take Back the Night*, New York: William Morrow, pp. 134–40.

Murray, William (1972) 'Interview: Sam Peckinpah', *Playboy* vol. 19 no. 8, August, pp. 65–74, 192; reprinted in Kevin J. Hayes (ed.) (2008) *Sam Peckinpah Interviews*, Jackson: University Press of Mississippi, pp. 96–120.

Novak, Glenn (2002) Email to Peter Woods, 13 March 2002.

Petley, Julian (2002) '"A Crude Sort of Entertainment for a Crude Sort of Audience": The British Critics and Horror Cinema', in Steve Chibnall and Julian Petley (eds) *British Horror Cinema*, London: Routledge.

Petley, Julian (2011) *Film and Video Censorship in Contemporary Britain*, Edinburgh: Edinburgh University Press.

Phelps, Guy (1975) *Film Censorship,* London: Victor Gollancz.

Phillips, McCandlish (1971) 'US Filmmakers De-emphasizing Sex', *New York Times*, 20 April, pp. 1, 48.

Pinter, Harold (2001) Email to Peter Woods, 25 September.

Prince, Stephen (1998) *Savage Cinema: Sam Peckinpah and the Rise of Ultraviolent Movies*, Austin: University of Texas Press.

Projansky, Sarah (2001) *Watching Rape: Film and Television in Postfeminist Culture*, New York: New York University Press.

Ruuth, Marianne [translator] (1972) *Sydsvenska Dagbladet Snallposten*, 25 April, pp. 1–5.

Sandbrook, Dominic (2006) *White Heat: A History of Britain in the Swinging Sixties*, London: Little, Brown.

Simmons, Garner (1998) *Peckinpah: A Portrait in Montage*, first published 1976, New York: Limelight Editions.

Slasherama.com [undated], 'Back from the Dead'. Available from: http://www.slasherama.com/features/zombie.HTML [accessed 26 June 2009].

Starr, Marco (1984) 'J. Hills Is Alive: A Defence of *I Spit on Your Grave*', in Martin Barker (ed.) *Video Nasties: Freedom and Censorship in the Media*, London: Pluto Press.

Swain, Jon (2008) 'The Truth about Men Who Kill', *Sunday Times*, new review section, 20 January, p. 7.

Thomson, David (2002) *Independent on Sunday*, 29 September, p. 11.

Travis, Alan (2002) 'Straw Dogs Video Ban Lifted', *Guardian*, 2 July 2002. Available from: http://www.guardian.co.uk/uk/2002/jul/02/media.filmnews [accessed 16 February 2011].

Trevelyan, John (1973) *What the Censor Saw*, London: Michael Joseph.

Walker, Alexander (1985) *National Heroes: British Cinema in the Seventies and Eighties*, London: Harrop.

Warga, Wayne (1972) 'Newest Bird to Brighten up Screen', *Los Angeles Times,* 27 February.

Weddle, David (1996) *Sam Peckinpah: 'If They Move ... Kill 'Em!'*, London: Faber and Faber.

Whittam Smith, Andreas (1999) Interview in the *Guardian*, 11 September. Available from: http://www.cultsock.ndirect.co.uk/MUHome/cshtml/media/bbfcdec.html [accessed July 17 2006].

Whittam Smith, Andreas and Robin Duval (1999) *Straw Dogs* statement, 2 June. Available from: http://www.bbfc.co.uk/news/press/19990602.html [accessed 14 July 2008].

Williams, Gordon (2003a) *Straw Dogs; Formerly: The Siege of Trencher's Farm*, first published 1969, London: Secker & Warburg.

Williams, Gordon (2003b) Interview. Available from: http://www.sundayherald.com/print31037 [accessed 1 September 2003].

Williams, Linda Ruth (1995) 'Women Only Can Misbehave: Peckinpah's *Straw Dogs*, Feminism and Violence', *Sight and Sound* vol. 5 no. 2, pp. 26–7.

Woods, Peter (2002) 'Last Appeal on the Left'. Available from: http://www.melonfarmers.co.uk/arbwlhotl.htm [accessed 25 February 2009].

Section 2: Sources from the Sam Peckinpah Collection, Margaret Herrick Library, Los Angeles

Numbers and letters in square brackets refer to the Peckinpah Collection folders

Anon (1970a) Notes taken at meeting with Dan Melnick 25 July [29-f.53].

Anon (James Swann's secretary) (1970b) Memo to Production Office, 22 December [f.28-37].

Anon (1971a) Undated Typed Script Notes on *Trencher's Farm* (unnamed, but calculations in Peckinpah's handwriting on reverse) [28-f.31].

Anon (1971b) Notes taken at script meeting held on 9 January with Sam Peckinpah, Dustin Hoffman, Susan George and David Goodman [28-f.31].

Anon (1971c) Undated notes on pub scenes (probably January) [29-f.52].

Anon (1971d) Undated memo (probably end of January) [29-f.61].

Anon (1971e) Sheet headed 'Artistic Freedom: Restraints and Responsibilities'. Outlines discussion topics for panel of that name at LA County Museum, 9 November.

Blevins, Winfred (1971) '"Straw Dogs": Peckinpah's Assault on Pacifism', *Los Angeles Herald Examiner*, 19 December, pp. F-1, F-4 [29-f.69].

Canby, Vincent (1972a) 'Peckinpah's "Straw Dogs" Starring Hoffman Arrives', *New York Times*, 20 January [29-f.69].

Canby, Vincent (1972b) 'The Ratings Are Wrong', *New York Times*, 4 June, pp. 1, 18 [29-f.69].

Carroll, Kathleen (1972) '"Straw Dogs" Orgy of Violence', *Daily News*, 20 January [29-f.69].

Cocks, Jay (1971) 'Peckinpah: Primitive Horror', *Time*, 20 December, pp. 85–7 [29-f.69].

Cook, Bruce (1972) 'The Sex and Violence Are Justified in Peckinpah's Tense "Straw Dogs"', *National Observer*, 15 January [29-f.69].

Doyle, Brian (1971) Publicity material [29-f.65].

Farber, Stephen and Estelle Changas (1972) 'Putting the Hex on "R" and "X"', *New York Times*, 9 April, Section 2, p. 1, cols 2–5 and p. 15, cols 1–5 [28-f.40].

Goodman, David Z. (1970a) Script Screenplay, *The Siege at Trencher's Farm* (no date: 1970?) [26-f.1].

Goodman, David Z. (1970b) Letter to Peckinpah, dated only 'Wednesday' (August 1970?) [28-f.46].

Goodman, David Z. and Sam Peckinpah (1970a) Screenplay, Corrected First Draft, *The Siege at Trencher's Farm*, 29 June; incomplete; heavily annotated by Peckinpah [27-f.4].

Goodman, David Z. and Sam Peckinpah (1970b) Script, *The Siege at Trencher's Farm*, rewritten pages of the first draft, part 1, April–July; many pages heavily annotated by Peckinpah [26-f.2].

Goodman, David Z. and Sam Peckinpah (1970c) Script, *The Siege at Trencher's Farm*, rewritten pages of the first draft, part 2, April–July; many pages heavily annotated by Peckinpah [26-f.3].

Goodman, David Z. and Sam Peckinpah (1970d) Script, *The Siege at Trencher's Farm*, rewritten and revised pages, various dates, first set of four, 30 June [28-f.26].

Goodman, David Z. and Sam Peckinpah (1970e) Script: Second Draft Corrected Proof Screenplay, *The Siege at Trencher's Farm*, 6 July, with changes to 3 August [27-f.6].

Goodman, David Z. and Sam Peckinpah (1970f) Script: Corrected Second Draft Screenplay, *The Siege at Trencher's Farm*, 5 August, medium annotations by Peckinpah [27-f.9].

Goodman, David Z. and Sam Peckinpah (1970g) Script: Draft, *The Siege at Trencher's Farm*, 22 October, with changes to 25 October (NB: noted as 'By Sam Peckinpah') [27-f.12].

Goodman, David Z. and Sam Peckinpah (1970h) Script, *The Siege at Trencher's Farm*, final mimeo typewritten script, before 24 November [27-f.14].

Goodman, David Z. and Sam Peckinpah (1970i) Script, *The Siege at Trencher's Farm*, revised and rewritten pages, fourth set of four, 21 December 1970 to 11 January 1971 [28-f.29].

Goodman, David Z. and Sam Peckinpah (1970j) Script, *The Siege at Trencher's Farm*, revised and rewritten pages, second set of four, 24 November 1970 to 24 January 1971 [28-f.27].

Goodman, David Z. and Sam Peckinpah (1971a) Script, *The Siege at Trencher's Farm*, final draft with progression of rewrites during shooting to 21 February, part 2 [27-f.19].

Goodman, David Z. and Sam Peckinpah (1971b) Script, *The Siege at Trencher's Farm*, final shooting script, 24 November 1970, with changes to 24 February, part 1 [27-f.20].

Goodman, David Z. and Sam Peckinpah (1971c) Script, *The Siege at Trencher's Farm*, final as-shot shooting script, 24 November 1970 to 24 February 1971 [28-f.21].

Hodenfield, Chris (1971) 'Sam Peckinpah Breaks a Bottle', *Rolling Stone* 13 May, no. 82, p. 12 [29-f.67].

Kavanagh, Derek (1970) Memo to James Swann cc: Peckinpah, 19 August [29-f.53].

Knickerbocker, Paine (1971) 'An Electrifying Film on Violence', *San Francisco Chronicle*, 23 December [29-f69].

Melnick, Dan (1970a) Undated notes, probably July [29-f.53].

Melnick, Dan (1970b) Memo to Peckinpah, 26 July [29-f.53].

Melnick, Dan (1970c) Cable to Peckinpah, 1 September [29-f.53].

Melnick, Dan (1971a) Memo to Peckinpah, 18 January [29-f.54].

Melnick, Dan (1971b) Memo to Peckinpah, 8 April [29-f.53].

Melnick, Dan (1971c) Memo to Peckinpah, 28 October [28-f.44].

Peckinpah, Sam (1970a) Letter to Martin Baum, 16 November [28-f.46].

Peckinpah, Sam (1970b) Cable to Dan Melnick, 2 September [29-f.53].

Peckinpah, Sam (1970c) Letter to David Warner in the Royal Orthopaedic Hospital, Great Portland St, London, 2 November [28-f.46].

Peckinpah, Sam (1970d) Letter to Martin Baum, 16 November [28-f.46].

Peckinpah, Sam (1970e) Letter to Harold Pinter, 11 December [28-f.46].

Peckinpah, Sam (1971a) Stapled sheaf of paper notes on reels, undated and unpaginated [28-f.44].

Peckinpah, Sam (1971b) Cable to Martin Baum, 10 January [28-f.44].

Peckinpah, Sam (1971c) Memo to Ken Hutchison, 1 March [29-f.54].

Peckinpah, Sam (1971d) Memo to Dan Melnick about Susan George, 15 March [29-f.53].

Peckinpah, Sam (1971e) Telex to Lew Rachmil, 30 March [28-f.44].

Peckinpah, Sam (1971f) Memo to Dan Melnick, 7 April [29-f.53].

Peckinpah, Sam (1971g) Letter to George Melly in response to his article of 28 November 'about my film Straw Dogs', undated (November/December) [29-f.65].

Peckinpah, Sam (1971h) Letter to Pauline Kael, undated [29-f.65].

Peckinpah, Sam (1971i) Draft letter to Richard Schickel, undated [29-f.65].

Peckinpah, Sam (1972a) Letter of reply to Miss Mary E. Scott of Baltimore, MD, 5 January [29-f.65].

Peckinpah, Sam (1972b) Letter in New York Times, published 7 May [28-f.40].

Pinter, Harold (1970) Letter to Sam Peckinpah, 9 December [28-f.46].

Rachmil, Lewis J. (1971a) Memo to Peckinpah and Melnick, 20 April [28-f.44].

Rachmil, Lewis J. (1971b) Memo to Peckinpah, 23 April [29-f.61].

Rachmil, Lewis J. (1971c) Editing notes to Peckinpah, 16 June [28-f.44].

Rachmil, Lewis J. (1971d) Editing notes to Peckinpah, 8 July [28-f.44].

Stern, Aaron (1972) Letter from Aaron Stern to Peckinpah, 11 April [28-f.40].

Swann, James (1971) Memo to Peckinpah, 22 April [29-f.61].

Valenti, Jack (1971) 'In Defense of the Voluntary Film Rating Program', *Harper's Bazaar*, July.

Walker, Beverly (1971) Letter to Peckinpah, 24 October [29-f.65]

Weitzner, David (1971) Cable to Peckinpah, 6 January [28-f.46]

Yardley, Jonathan (1971) '"Straw Dogs": Finest Movie of 1971', *Greensboro Daily News*, 23 December, p. B19 [29-f.67].

Yergin, Dan (1971) 'Wildest of the Bunch', *Daily Telegraph Magazine* no. 359, 10 September, pp. 32–9 [29-f.67].

Zimmerman, Paul D. (1971) 'Rites of Manhood', *Newsweek*, 20 December, p. 87 [29-f.69].

Section 3: Sources from the Archive of the British Board of Film Classification, London

Anon (1971) Internal note from BBFC examiners on *Straw Dogs*, 3 November.

Cashin, Fergus (1972) 'Terror Films Shock Critics', *Sun*, 7 January.

Gibbs, Patrick (1971) 'Shooting It Out with the Limeys', *Straw Dogs* review, November.

Hanley, Pam (2000) *Sense and Sensibilities: Public Opinion & the BBFC Guidelines*. Available from: http://www.bbfc.co.uk/download/guidelines/2000%20Guidelines %20Research%20-%20Sense%20and%20Sensibilities.pdf [accessed 16 February 2011].

Hinxman, Margaret (1971) 'Blood and Blunder', *Straw Dogs* review, *Sunday Telegraph*, 28 November.

Melly, George (1971) 'Mixing Sex and Violence', review of *Straw Dogs*, *Observer*, November.

Melnick, Dan (1971) Letter to Stephen Murphy, 19 August.

Murphy, Stephen (1971a) Letter to Dan Melnick, 10 November.

Murphy, Stephen (1971b) Letter to RCB, 7 December.

Murphy, Stephen (1972) Letter to RCB, 7 February.

Murphy, Stephen and Lord Harlech (1971) Letter to *The Times*, 20 December.

Powell, Dilys (1971) 'The Cinema in Danger', *Straw Dogs* review, *The Times*, 28 November.

RCB (1972) Letter to Stephen Murphy, 5 February.

Robinson, David (1971) 'The Instinctive Censor', *Financial Times*, 26 November.

Walker, Alexander (1971) 'After This, Anything Goes ...', review of *Straw Dogs*, *Evening Standard*, 26 November.

Section 4: DVD editions used as references

Straw Dogs, DVD, Fremantle Home Entertainment edition, released 7 October 2002 (UK).

Straw Dogs, DVD, Criterion Collection edition, released 25 March 2003 (US).

Straw Dogs – Wer Gewalt sat ..., DVD, EuroVideo edition, released 12 July 2007 (Germany).

Index